LEADERSPRITZ

LEADERSPRITZ

THE INTERPERSONAL LEADERSHIP COCKTAIL

Marianne Schmid Mast, PhD
Tristan Palese, PhD
Benjamin Tur, PhD

EPFL PRESS

This book is published under the editorial direction of Professor Jean-Philippe Bonardi.

The cover was created by Eric Garence. Artist and poster designer, he realizes art illustrations for the Principality of Monaco, the brand Côte d'Azur France, the Galeries Lafayette, Fragonard but also for authors such as Gérard A. Jaeger, Swiss historian, essayist and novelist. Follow his news and exhibitions: www.ericgarence.com

Graphic design and layout: Kim Nanette

EPFL PRESS

is an imprint owned by the Foundation Presses polytechniques et universitaires romandes (PPUR), a Swiss academic publishing company whose main purpose is to publish the teaching and research works of the Ecole polytechnique fédérale de Lausanne (EPFL), of universities and other institutions of higher education.
PPUR, EPFL – Rolex Learning Center, CP 119, CH-1015 Lausanne, info@epflpress.org

www.epflpress.org

First edition
ISBN 978-2-88915-387-9
© EPFL PRESS / Presses polytechniques et universitaires romandes, 2020

Printed in Italy

Contents

An Introduction to Leaderspritz:
A Scientific Cocktail

This book is for women and men in leadership positions, as well as for those who aspire to such positions. Its purpose? To enable you to become an expert in social interactions, capable of managing your staff and your current and future responsibilities.

Our philosophy is simple; just as the *spritz* requires a balanced—almost scientific—blend of ingredients to become a refreshing and light cocktail, leadership is a skillful blend of sensitivity, competence, and expertise. Using practical tools, anecdotes, empirical results, and scientific theories, this book aims to provide a reading firmly grounded in facts, but that is also enjoyable and entertaining.

Unlike books that give subjective advice or biographies of famous leaders, this book is based on rigorous scientific research. In contrast to personal experiences, which are certainly edifying, but always singular, the tools presented here stem from solid empirical evidence and are therefore generalizable beyond the individual case. In other words, there is no bias related to small sample size.

Imagine a Japanese tourist on vacation in the Swiss Alps witnessing the *désalpe* (a traditional festival during which cows, decorated with flower crowns and heavy bells, descend from the mountain pastures to the plain). Is this sample sufficient to learn about the lifestyle of Swiss cows? In the mind of the passing tourist, will Swiss cows always be adorned with flowers? Such a conclusion would be as hasty as it is far from reality... Yet the same is true for books based on the personal experience of particular leaders, true in their case, but impossible to generalize to all. Scientific studies, however, testing the effectiveness or occurrence of certain behaviors on samples of several hundred people make it possible to avoid such biases.

Another advantage of a science-based book is that the behaviors described have been shown to be effective. Unlike empirical studies, books based on personal experiences very rarely measure the effect of a specific behavior or habit on performance. Yes, a leader's success can be used as a performance indicator; but how to identify among all of the leader's particularities and actions those that have really determined his or her success? How can you be sure that drinking a glass of hot water with lemon (certainly very healthy), removing the door to your office, or developing a certain competency recommended by a famous leader is really the determining factor?

Finally, a science-based book on leadership gives readers greater credibility among those surrounding them. Developing leadership skills is not an easy endeavor and should not be undertaken alone. It is a difficult path for which leaders need not only the support of their collaborators, but also a willingness on behalf of their superiors to invest in the development of their skills. The scientific studies described in this book provide justification for the need to develop certain skills. If the experience of a successful leader can serve as inspiration, it is essential to have objective and quantifiable facts to address the challenges related to your being or becoming an efficient and successful leader.

This book can be savored like a cocktail, where and how you like it best. You can read it at a sidewalk café, on a couch, in a library, while travelling, alone, or with others. Only one thing really matters, starting at the beginning and learning, step by step, how to become an expert in social interactions.

1 Why Are Leaders Important?

On August 5, 2010, the San José copper mine in Chile collapsed on thirty-three men. Teams from all over the world were mobilized, taking turns to help rescue the survivors. Seventeen days later, a note arrived at the surface: *"Estamos bien el refugio, los 33."* All the miners were safe but trapped more than two thousand feet underground. Sixty-nine days later, Luis Urzúa was the last man to leave the mine.

Although the miners were saved by the rescue teams, the survival of the thirty-three men owed a lot to Urzúa. As the person responsible for the shift he was the one to coordinate efforts, encourage his men not to give up, and establish a hierarchy by assigning roles based on skills and personality. Florencio Ávalos was appointed second-in-command. Yonni Barrios, who had spent six months at his sick mother's bedside, became the group's doctor. Mario Gómez, the oldest, took on the role of spiritual leader and organized prayer times. Mario Sepúlveda, a cheerful and dynamic person, produced a video diary to reassure the families of the trapped. In a few days, the group structured itself into a hierarchy around its leader.

The story of Luis Urzúa and the Chilean miners is not unique. As soon as a group of people comes together, one or more leaders emerge and a hierarchy is established, often in just a few minutes. As in the case of the Chilean miners, small differences are used, often unconsciously, to assign roles within the group. Behaviors, specific knowledge, personality, where a person sits around a table, age or physical appearance: anything can be used to distribute tasks and responsibilities. But why do humans systematically create hierarchies?

The Origin of Hierarchies

Strength comes from unity. This maxim describes in a simple way the evolutionary strategy of many animal species, showing that living together increases the chances of survival. Antelopes, oryx, and even some fish move in groups to improve their chances at spotting predators (fifty eyes are better than two) and escaping from them. Other species, such as wild geese or ibises, fly in formation to optimize their energy consumption and aerodynamics. Still others gather in groups to hunt larger and therefore more nutritious prey. This is particularly the case for wolves and lions.

By choosing to live together, these "social" species enjoy some benefits, but they are also faced with a new challenge: coordination. Imagine for a moment a pack of wolves chasing a moose without coordinating their actions. They all start to pursue their meal, the fastest in front, the slowest at the back. If the moose has done its cardio workouts properly, it will exhaust its predators and come out of the chase alive. However, if the pack is organized, it will be more dangerous than just its fastest members. Some wolves will force the prey in one direction, while others will cut it off, the whole becoming more effective than the sum of its parts. The assignment of clear roles and the adoption of a hierarchy allows social species to solve important problems such as maximizing access to food sources and minimizing the chances of ending up on someone else's plate.

The human species is, of course, a social species. Like wolves, living in a group has increased our chances of survival, but we have also needed to develop coordination strategies. Hierarchies speed up the group's decision-making process, help to manage conflict, and minimize the risk of diffusion of responsibility.

Imagine being confronted with an unconscious person lying in a crowded street. Would you stop to help the person, or would you continue on your way as if nothing had happened? Chances are that you will take the second option. Why? Like most people, you will probably think that someone else will help. In October 2011, some twenty people passed by a two-year-old girl, Wang Yue, who was dying by the roadside after being run over by a car. A woman finally stopped, unfortunately too late to save the girl. Could this tragic event have been avoided if a hierarchy and clear roles had been established between bystanders on the street? Probably. Law enforcement officials recommend that victims of assault single out a bystander and ask for this person's assistance, rather than shout "Help!" without targeting a specific person. In companies, this phenomenon of diffusion of responsibility is observed when several employees work on a project without defined responsibilities. Everyone thinks that someone else will contact the supplier and, in the end, no one does. Hierarchies make it possible to clarify everyone's responsibilities and therefore avoid misunderstandings with potentially disastrous consequences.

However, human societies have evolved; we have developed new forms of organization and communication, as well as new technological means of information exchange. In view of these changes, one might wonder whether hierarchies are still necessary for the proper functioning of a group. Aren't they the remnants of a bygone past?

Should We Remove Hierarchies?

Removing hierarchical structures and getting rid of managers are new trends adopted by both international organizations and local SMEs. The media frequently publishes articles announcing the end of hierarchies in companies. The term used is "holacracy" or horizontal organization. The removal of hierarchies is driven by a desire to accelerate decision-making and to give employees more autonomy. This levels so-called formal hierarchies, which are illustrated by the titles on business cards or positions in organizational charts: CEO, CFO, Head of Sales, etc. Each position has its responsibilities and powers, its ways of being rewarded and punished.

In 2002, Google got rid of all engineering management positions. The company wanted to give employees more time to work on their projects, while saving time previously spent supervising staff performance. After a few months, there was a long line of people waiting outside the office of Larry Page, one of Google's founders. The reasons? There were relational conflicts to resolve, decisions to approve, and resources to allocate between departments. Google had just discovered that hierarchies could not be removed completely. The experiment was short-lived. Eleven years later, Google still has 5,000 managers and 37,000 employees. Their new strategy? Less pronounced but more relevant hierarchical levels.

Google's experience illustrates a contradiction. On the one hand, the desire to gain time and autonomy by flattening hierarchies; on the other hand, the almost primitive need to refer to a superior to solve interpersonal conflicts, ensure coordination, and allocate resources and responsibilities. As a matter of fact, even in the absence of a formal hierarchy, an informal hierarchy forms systematically with one or more leaders emerging at its head. Those leadership positions are not defined through the usual organizational charts, promotions, or formal appointments, they emerge around certain skills, personalities, or competencies important for the group. The question is therefore not whether there should be hierarchies—there always will be—but what makes hierarchies effective.

At the Top of the Hierarchy

At first glance, certain types of hierarchies are better suited for some contexts than others. In crisis situations, involving rapid decisions and potentially serious consequences, hierarchies are very often formal and strict. This is particularly the case for surgical operations, anti-terrorist interventions, and firefighting. These contexts involve special *modus operandi*, that is, predefined methods of action, known to group members and applied under supervision.

In other contexts, such as in the corporate world, the trend is to advocate less pronounced hierarchies in order to foster innovation and performance. But are these more horizontal structures really favorable? Studies present contradictory results. Sometimes, performance improves with flatter hierarchies, sometimes it diminishes. According to some researchers, flat hierarchies are more effective when tasks require increased information sharing between group members. However, we have recently carried out a study that invalidates this idea. Our results showed that the type of hierarchy, pronounced or flat, was not related to the group's performance. The real predictor of performance is not how steep a hierarchy is, but who the person emerging as its leader is. If the leader is competent, the group's performance increases significantly, regardless of the hierarchical structure in place.

To have the best leaders, companies invest billions each year to train their executives. Companies such as

Nestlé or Credit Suisse have developed dedicated training centers for their senior managers. Other companies are implementing ever more innovative initiatives to identify the people best suited to be leaders in their teams. W. L. Gore, the company that developed Gore-Tex, for example, has set up a new type of organization. The divisions and departments are clearly established but the leader role is not assigned, it emerges naturally. In other words, each collaborator can propose a project and provide leadership if he or she obtains the support of their colleagues. Employees are thus appointed by their peers to guide them.

Whatever the approach, one thing is clear, leadership is a central preoccupation for many organizations. The stakes are high, and the people promoted need valuable tools to face the challenges ahead.

2 The Fourteen-Billion-Dollar Question

It took place in November. We had just hosted a conference for alumni of the Faculty of Business and Economics at the University of Lausanne, Switzerland. These were professionals returning to a classroom in their former university for just one evening. During the informal gathering and networking at the cocktail reception, a moment when we juggle between holding appetizers, hanging on to our wine glasses, and shaking hands, a young woman approached us. She briefly introduced herself and explained that she had just been promoted within her company. This new leadership position was putting her under considerable stress. Experienced in her field but a novice leader, she wanted to obtain expert advice. She was looking for answers and the tools to succeed, or at least to not fail, in her new role. Ultimately, what she really wanted to know was: What makes a good leader?

This was not the first time we had been asked the question, whether by team leaders, human resources managers, or students. Answering it is as tricky and dangerous as explaining what makes a good parent. Is the "success" of a parent measured by the happiness of their children, their grades at school, or the prestige of their future profession? Is being a good parent gauged by the quality of the relationship the parents have with their children? By the amount of time parents and kids spend together? Can parents be excellent in the eyes of their children and mediocre in the eyes of other parents?

It is equally difficult to pinpoint the qualities of a good leader. Should we consider the well-being of our employees, the turnover rate in our company, or the quality of our relationships with our employees? Should leader success be measured in terms of how much impact leaders have in their respective fields, be it in a company, an association, a political party, or a sports club? Does a surgeon need the same leadership skills as a bank manager? Can a political leader be considered excellent in one country and bad in another? The question of the qualities of a good leader is as broad as it is tentacular. So where should we start?

What Does a Leader Do?

To find the starting point, let's rephrase this young woman's question. Instead of asking what makes a good leader, we can ask what it is that a leader does throughout a busy day. Indeed, how can we define the characteristics of a good leader if we do not know the tasks a leader is confronted with? In other words, what is it that leaders spend their time on?

This seemingly simple question was asked in the 1970s by Henry Minzberg, a professor at McGill University in Montreal (and a keen collector of beaver sculptures...), one of the pioneers in research on leadership. Imitated later on by other researchers, he accompanied business leaders for several days, meticulously observing and transcribing their daily activities. The results of these observations show that leaders' activities can be grouped into twelve categories:

1. Plan and coordinate
2. Manage staff
3. Train and develop
4. Make decisions and solve problems
5. Perform administrative tasks
6. Exchange routine information
7. Monitor performance
8. Motivate and strengthen
9. Discipline and punish
10. Interact with external actors
11. Manage conflicts
12. Socialize and network

Up until then, leadership had been seen as a succession of strategic reflections, whiteboards covered with Post-it notes, or performance monitoring. Minzberg's study revealed a very different face of leadership. Indeed, these activities actually represent only 20 percent of a leader's time, the remaining 80 percent being dedicated to... social interactions.

WHAT LEADERSHIP LOOKS LIKE

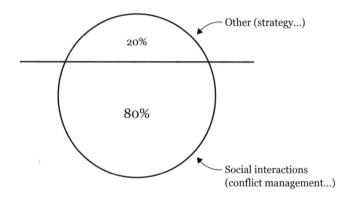

Social interactions refer to all types of exchanges between several people. A leader therefore spends on average 80 percent of their time communicating with others, such as collaborators, customers, suppliers, stakeholders, or other leaders. James Humes, the famous speechwriter for five US presidents, wisely said: "The art of communication is the language of leadership." This statement is even more telling when we consider the results of studies conducted by researchers at the universities of Nebraska, Illinois, and Florida. These show that the more time leaders spend on social interactions (talking to collaborators, managing conflicts, networking, etc.), the more they excel in the leadership role.

Technical, strategic, and operational skills are, of course, important. After all, like the young woman at the cocktail reception, most people are promoted because they shine in their profession. However, by being promoted, one accepts a new suit and a new role. Being a leader is first and foremost being an expert in social interactions. And, to succeed in this domain, you must not only be able to make yourself understood, but you must also listen in order to understand others. How many leaders have learned this lesson the hard way?

In 1977, two commercial airliners collided on the tarmac at Tenerife airport, killing 583 people. Could the pilot have avoided this crash by listening more carefully to his co-pilots? In 1985, Steve Jobs was fired from his own company. Would he have avoided this crisis if he had managed his employees differently? In 2017, Marine Le Pen lost the race for the French presidency after a catastrophic televised debate. Would she have been elected if she had chosen another communication style? Answering these questions implies asking another one first: Can leaders learn to better manage social interactions? Or, more generally: Can leadership be learned?

Can You Learn to Become a Good Leader?

Is leadership innate or acquired? The debate has animated the scientific world for years. The issue is not only important for science but also for the private sector, which invests huge amounts (nearly fourteen billion per year in the United States) to train its leaders. Would it really be appropriate for companies to spend that amount if leadership was just a matter of innate talent?

We speak of "innate" to refer to stable personal characteristics—therefore difficult to change—over time and across different contexts. This is the case, for example, for personality traits. In principle, outgoing people will easily reach out to others throughout their entire lifespan and in many different situations. Talent can be innate, such as in people who have perfect pitch in music. "Acquired" refers to behaviors and skills that can be learned and trained. You learn to read a balance sheet in accounting, to speak Mandarin, or to develop a strategic vision.

With regard to leadership, science clearly shows that it is a mixture of innate and acquired skills. Although intelligence or certain personality traits contribute to a leader's success, other factors also come into play. A study conducted with senior managers has shown that charisma, and therefore the power of persuasion, can be learned! This does not mean, however, that we are all starting on a level playing field. Just as Usain Bolt (whose natural height advantage allows him to run the 100 meters in forty-one strides compared to forty-four for a medium-sized human being) was born with a predisposition for his sport, some people are naturally better equipped for leadership.

However, in the same way that athletes increase their speed by training, it is possible to improve one's leadership skills. Investing in executive training therefore makes sense for companies, and especially investing in interpersonal skills training for leaders, who spend 80 percent of their time managing social interactions.

3 The Science of Communication

Sophia is a senior consultant. She works in Switzerland but sometimes has to travel for work. Today, she has just landed at Tokyo Narita Airport in Japan (this story takes place in a pre-COVID-19 world) and decides to go directly to her company's offices to get to know her team. When she enters the meeting room, she recognizes a few faces from the intranet photos. She walks up to these people and reaches out her hand. After three long seconds, she realizes with embarrassment that no one is taking it. Her Japanese collaborators exchange a few puzzled glances and respectfully bend over.

This situation—definitely awkward—is certainly a cliché, but it is representative of the many social faux pas that can happen. Often dogged by cameras, politicians provide an inexhaustible wealth of examples. During a visit to Senegal, Emmanuel Macron (the acting French president) confused his wife's hand with that of the Senegalese president and walked hand-in-hand with him for a few meters before realizing his error. During a visit to Germany, François Hollande (another French president) and Angela Merkel (Germany's well-known chancellor) bumped into each other several times trying to coordinate their movements as they visited the troops. Although these situations are embarrassing for the people concerned, they are ultimately without consequences. Other misunderstandings, on the contrary, can have much more disastrous consequences. In July 1945, the war in Europe ended and all eyes were turned to Japan. Allied leaders met in Potsdam. They sent an ultimatum to the Japanese government: unconditional surrender or war and destruction. When asked by journalists what his reply to the ultimatum was, Kantaro Suzuki said: "Mokusatsu." Derived from the word "silence," this word can have several meanings. When the Japanese prime minister said it, what he meant was "no comment." However, in the eyes of the Allies, the answer sounded like "unworthy of comment." The decision to bomb Hiroshima and Nagasaki therefore resulted, among other things, from a simple misunderstanding.

Communicate with Words and the Body

As we have seen, social interactions occupy 80 percent of leaders' time. They affect the company's performance and the quality of human relationships at work. Learning to manage the many social situations that characterize our day-to-day life is therefore essential for improving our leadership skills. Becoming a communication expert requires two kinds of expertise: verbal and nonverbal.

Verbal communication refers to the words we use. It includes the choice of words, the structure of our sentences, and the logic of our arguments. When the Japanese prime minister said "Mokusatsu" at the end of the Second World War, it was verbal communication. Nonverbal communication includes all other forms of information transmission. The palette is as wide as it is diversified, ranging from voice intonation to gestures and including eye contact and clothing. Nonverbal behaviors can be divided into two distinct families according to whether they are related to speech production (voice modulation, speech volume, hesitations, including the ubiquitous "um" when searching for words, etc.) or not (posture, gestures, actions of looking, facial expressions, appearance, etc.). Most of our daily social interactions combine verbal and nonverbal communication. This considerably facilitates our exchanges. If you tell someone to go left and point in that direction, you reduce the chances of the other person turning right.

Which of the two languages takes precedence over the other? It's all about context. In Sophia's case, nonverbal communication was predominant because it seems to be at the root of the misunderstanding. In contrast, words are essential for the presentation of annual results by a CFO. Finally, verbal and nonverbal communication can be of equal importance, such as a smile accompanying the ironic statement "What a beautiful day!" against the backdrop of a storm. Be careful, therefore, with the urban legend suggesting that 93 percent of communication is nonverbal: it is all a matter of context.

The Yin and the Yang of Communication

Leaders interpret others' behaviors and express behaviors themselves. Within a single interaction, they change hat several times, just like Sophia. When she entered the meeting room, she began to express herself by reaching out her hand, then tried to interpret the reaction of her collaborators, before finally expressing herself again by bending over, blushing. Expression and understanding are complementary and interdependent: the Yin and the Yang of communication. Imagine the financial director of a hospital addressing the department heads, most of them doctors. In order to provide them with useful and accessible information, his eloquence and the well-prepared slides will not be enough. He will have to understand their expectations and capture their reactions as he speaks. If he is not able to decipher the puzzled looks when they hear the word "EBITDA," he will not bother to explain that it is earnings before interest, taxes, depreciation, and amortization, and will definitely lose the attention of the doctors present in the audience. The latter may be able to perform open-heart surgery, but they do not necessarily have the accounting skills to understand its acronyms and related financial jargon.

Yin corresponds to the way of transmitting the message you want to communicate. We also talk about encoding. It is based on both verbal and nonverbal behavior. You can choose simple words, technical words, or metaphors. You can speak in a low voice, normally, or scream.

THE YIN AND THE YANG
OF INTERPERSONAL COMMUNICATION

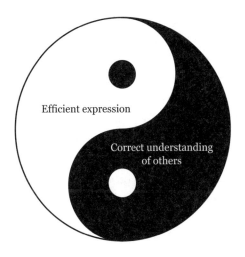

You can even manipulate your appearance to transmit your message. It is therefore not uncommon for heads of state to adapt their clothing style to the message they want to convey. In the United States, George W. Bush and Barack Obama both wore military jackets to address the troops during their terms. In France, Emmanuel Macron donned a pilot suit during a visit to Istres Air Force Base in July 2017, inspiring a "Made in France" *Top Gun* remake. In all of these cases, the goal was the same: to demonstrate their role as army leaders. Canadian Prime Minister Justin Trudeau chose to wear traditional Indian clothing during his diplomatic visit to the Taj Mahal in February 2018 to express his appreciation for the country.

Yang, or decoding, refers to the interpretation of the verbal and nonverbal behavior of others. To complete Justin Trudeau's example, Indian public opinion judged his appearance as a clumsy, even disrespectful attempt to express his appreciation for Indian culture. If the Canadian Prime Minister—or his communications officers—had studied the culture more carefully, a different strategy would probably have been chosen. Similarly, an e-mail written in capital letters can be interpreted as a sign of irritation when it could simply be a handling error. A good encoder is first and foremost an excellent decoder. Leaders must therefore be able to interpret the behaviors of the people with whom they interact.

Reading Others Correctly—But How?

Imagine that, like Sophia at the beginning of this chapter, you are meeting your new team members for the first time. Right from the outset, you will observe their behavior and try to discern personalities, skills, ways of working, individual motivations, and the type and quality of the relationships they have with each other. The ability to correctly decode this information will enable all leaders to become more effective. People who are considered as being more serious and motivated will be given more responsibilities, various conflicts will be avoided by assigning joint projects to people who get along well, etc.

While some of us are naturally good with numbers or in sports, others have an above-average talent for decoding others. This is the case of John Yarbrough, an American police officer. Once, while on duty in Los Angeles with his teammate, Yarbrough approached a stationary car. A man jumped out and pointed his gun at him. They found themselves face to face, threatening each other with their weapons. The choice was simple: shoot each other Western style or not shoot and hope the other does the same. Yarbrough decided to lower his weapon. He was quickly imitated by the stranger, and the arrest was made without violence. When questioned by his superiors, Yarbrough said he knew that the other man was not dangerous and that he would not shoot.

The example of Yarbrough is interesting because it is exceptional. After conducting tests on his social skills, psychologists identified in the police officer an extraordinary ability to detect lies, a rare quality, even for a police officer. A study in the United States examined this competency by comparing members of the secret services, the FBI, as well as police officers, judges, psychiatrists, students, and ordinary adults. What was the result? Only members of the secret services were able to detect lies at a rate of accuracy above that of mere luck.

In our professional lives, and more generally in our everyday lives, perceiving others correctly necessitates being accurate in judging other people's personalities, emotions, motivations, or intentions. Unlike the detection of lies—an exceptional skill—the ability to understand others based on these aspects is more common. Of course, there are individual differences. Open, outgoing, and tolerant people are able to decode their social interaction partners better, probably simply because they are more frequently engaged in social interactions. Similarly, people who grow up with introverted and uncommunicative parents develop better decoding abilities as they learn to compensate for their parents' lack of expression by being hypersensitive to their behavior.

When Yarbrough decided to lower his weapon, he didn't know what the other person was going to do, but he recognized behaviors—a subtle facial expression, a look, a hesitation in the voice—that he interpreted as a sign that the person didn't want to pull the trigger. Even if you are not like Yarbrough, the good news is that it is possible to learn to decode others correctly. Unfortunately, we cannot offer such training here (this is typically done by studying various behaviors and expressions on videos accompanied by expert feedback), but we can give suggestions aimed at sharpening these interpersonal reading skills.

Imagine yourself in a meeting with business partners. They arrived in a pack of three in your office, all with the same title. It is therefore difficult to know whom to talk to first and, especially, to find out who the decision-maker is. Without further information, you will tend to address the person who looks at you directly, has a loud voice, approaches you first, gestures a lot, or puts their hand on your shoulder. Why? Because these are behaviors believed to be indicative of high status.

People thus use them frequently to find out who is the boss in a group of people they do not know.[1]

Are these behaviors reliable "symptoms" of leadership? Not all of them! In general, leaders can be recognized by a more open posture, a more expressive face, less interpersonal distance, a louder voice, more interruptions, more speaking time, and more visual dominance (which corresponds to looking at a person when you talk to them and not looking at them when they talk to you). Those are the behaviors that you should use to identify the person with the highest status among the three business partners.

Reading others correctly is an undeniable asset for a leader. Those who possess this skill, or have developed it, have more satisfied employees, higher salaries, and perform better in their jobs. However, if decoding, the leader's "fatal weapon," can be learned, why are we still so often wrong when making inferences about others? Probably because our brains tend to take shortcuts...

---

[1] Here is the complete list of nonverbal behaviors often used to try to detect who is the leader: more eye contact, fewer raised eyebrows, more expressive face, more nodding, less self-touching, more physical contact, more hand and arm gestures, more open posture, less relaxed posture, more posture changes, less interpersonal distance, more voice variations, louder voice, more interruptions, fewer pauses and less hesitation in speaking, faster speech rate, lower and more grounded voice, more speaking time, more visual dominance.

4 Can We Trust Our Brains?

Heuristics and Stereotypes

A father and son return from a skiing weekend in the Swiss Alps. They are quietly driving down the mountain when a driver coming from the opposite direction loses control over his vehicle and hits them at 50 mph. The father dies instantly. The son has a serious head injury. An ambulance takes him to the nearest hospital and a neurosurgeon specialist is flown in by helicopter. Upon entering the operating room, the neurosurgeon sees the child and says in a devastated voice: "I can't operate on this child; this is my son..." How is this possible?

When we ask this question during our training and university courses, the majority of participants conclude that the boy was adopted and that the specialist is his biological father. You may have come to the same conclusion. However, is this the most obvious solution? No. The most obvious answer is that it's his mother, a neurosurgeon. Even if the solution may seem simple, we generally need time and heavy thinking to achieve it. Why? Because our brain uses shortcuts that sometimes lead to wrong conclusions. A leader's mission involves understanding how these shortcuts or heuristics work, being aware of their consequences on our behaviors, and learning techniques to overcome them.

Heuristics

When we receive a message, our brain processes the information through what is called a cognitive network, meaning that it will seek to establish links with known elements in order to draw conclusions. A child who sees a flame for the first time will probably want to touch it. An adult will associate the flame with pain and be careful not to approach it. In both cases, the child and the adult use their knowledge to interpret information and make a decision. Our brain constantly uses this mechanism. When we hear someone screaming "Thief!" different concepts are automatically activated and emerge in front of our mental eye: black hood, evil look, feeling of danger, running man, etc. This association of concepts is an example of a cognitive network. Our brains weave these threads together almost instantly, so that when we hear the word "thief," we immediately look around trying to find the fleeing man, dressed in dark colors—all of this without having received the slightest description of the thief. A woman in a flowery dress, who escapes by walking calmly away, would most likely not be noticed because her characteristics are not linked to "thief" in our minds. This notion of cognitive networks also explains why it is difficult to solve the neurosurgeon riddle. The word "specialist," used to describe the person brought in by helicopter, is more frequently associated with a man, and the same is true for a neurosurgeon. By taking these shortcuts, our brain concludes that it has to be a man, and it is only by making a conscious effort to think carefully about the problem that we can find an alternative interpretation to solve the riddle.

Such shortcuts are referred to as heuristics, strategies enabling us to make decisions quickly, without necessarily having to process all the available information. Our mnid olny uess the frist and lsat ltteer of a wrod to unerdsntad the manenig of a snetnece. There is a heuristic right here: We see a word as a whole rather than as a given series of letters.

Often unconsciously, heuristics emerge in a wide variety of situations. Imagine for a moment recruiting a new employee after an interview. You only have partial information available and will have to base your decision on heuristics such as a degree from a renowned university (intellectual ability), a promotion on the CV (competent and appreciated applicant), a firm handshake (self-confidence).

In principle, heuristics are beneficial tools, mechanisms that save us time in decision-making. However, they are not always accurate. More often than not, they distort reality and lead to bad decisions with negative outcomes, such as hiring the wrong person based on a misleading first impression. Leaders need to be careful not to apply a particular type of heuristics—stereotypes.

What Is a Stereotype?

The Japanese are small. Blondes are stupid. Generation Y is lazy. The French are always on strike. These are stereotypes, characteristics attributed to a person simply because they belong to a certain social group. The Swiss, for example, have a reputation for always being on time, and the French are supposedly always late. But are the Swiss really more punctual than their neighbors? Or, to put it another way, do stereotypes represent reality or are they completely false? To answer this question, imagine yourself in front of a person who is a secretary, visualize the person... Got it?

What is the first image that came to your mind? Most likely that of a woman. Like most of us, you possess a stereotype about this profession. This stereotype is not due to the absence of male secretaries but rather to an under-representation of men in this profession. But even when some stereotypes are based on real, existing differences, they are a distortion of reality.

To illustrate this phenomenon, imagine yourself in an Airbus A380 filled with 50 percent Chinese people (known to be small) and 50 percent Dutch individuals (known to be tall). For obscure reasons (that do not concern us here), you decide to assess the height of all the passengers. This results in a distribution of how tall each person is on the horizontal axis and how many of the passengers correspond to each height measure on the vertical axis. The graph below represents this reality. On average, the Chinese in the plane measure 5.5 feet compared to 6.0 feet for the Dutch. As you can see, there is also a very tall Chinese man (6.3 feet; probably Li Chunjiang, a former basketball player) and a very small Dutch person (5.3 feet, probably a naturalized Chinese woman).

Two psychological mechanisms are at the root of stereotypes, resulting in them being a distortion of reality. The first mechanism is the exaggeration of the difference between the two groups. If we use our example again, the height gap between the Chinese and the Dutch is perceived as being greater than it really is. Relying on the stereotype, we think that the Chinese measure 5.2 feet when in reality they are 5.5 feet tall, and we think that the Dutch measure 6.2 feet when their average height is really 6.0 feet.

The second mechanism is a difference in perception between the group to which we belong and the group that is foreign to us. We generally perceive our own group as more diverse and the foreign group as much more homogeneous. This uniformity is reflected in the distribution: the narrower it is, the less diversity is perceived. A Dutchman will see all Chinese people as very small. But, for the same Dutchman, there are large and small fellow citizens, illustrated by a wider distribution for the Dutch in the lower graph.

Finally, other stereotypes are not based on any facts or statistics. They are pure fabrications of the collective imagination, like the so-called low intellectual capacities of blondes. Discriminating against blondes in order

REALITY

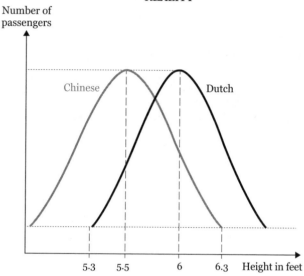

STEROTYPE

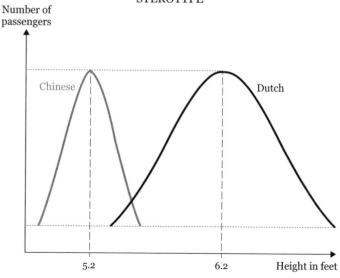

to ensure the hiring of intelligent collaborators is obviously a mistake. There are just as many intelligent brunettes, blondes, and redheads, and as the saying goes: "There are fools everywhere."

Where Do Stereotypes Come From?

At this point in the chapter, you might wonder why we use stereotypes at all if they are so misleading. There are two reasons. The first is evolutionary. Tens of thousands of years ago, the human species lived in small groups and anyone different or outside the group represented a potentially lethal danger. By associating stereotypes with foreign groups, we were able to recognize danger more quickly and thus increase our chances of survival. Even though the risk of being knocked out with a large rock when leaving the house has considerably decreased nowadays, our brains still hold on to these thousand-year-old mechanisms.

The second explanation is social. As a social species, we need to feel that we belong to a group. Therefore, we categorize, classify, and order our social environment into different groups with members of the same group sharing one or more characteristics. Holding a British passport puts us in the Brits social group. Being an entrepreneur puts us in the group of entrepreneurs. One person typically belongs to several different groups. Angela Merkel is simultaneously a woman, a politician, German, and a scientist (she has a doctorate in quantum chemistry). By identifying with a group, we develop our social identity, but we also exaggerate our differences with "foreign" groups; in other words, we create stereotypes.

The Consequences of Stereotypes

Stereotypes affect leaders on a very practical level. Due to the stereotype "Think Manager—Think Male," we tend, without even realizing it, to favor men for management positions. Because the leadership role is associated with male attributes, we prefer applicants who possess these traits. We also adapt our behavior to the candidate's gender, for example, by giving more speaking time to men than women during job interviews. To the extent that speaking time signals dominance, and therefore leadership, even a small difference in time talked can influence perception and thus who gets hired for the high-status position.

In addition, stereotypes (and we all have them) can affect the behavior of our interaction partners in such a way that they themselves—without wanting to—confirm our expectations. We think, for example, that our young collaborators are constantly engaged in social media. We will therefore send them more messages through this channel and they, wanting to please their superior, will be more responsive. The stereotype does not get confirmed because it is true, but because our behavior is guided unconsciously by it. This is called a self-fulfilling prophecy.

Given the power of stereotypes and the risk they entail, it is better for all those in a leadership position to decide and act on the basis of unbiased information. But, how can we achieve this, knowing that stereotypes are automatically activated and most of the time operate unconsciously?

How to Avoid Bias?

We use heuristics for a simple and good reason: unlike computers, our cognitive capacity is limited. In addition, the information we receive is often incomplete or insufficient and therefore requires us to make decisions in a context of uncertainty. It is impossible to live without heuristics, even if using such shortcuts exposes us to the risk of error. Some techniques, such as controlled cognition, nevertheless allow us to take advantage of heuristics while at the same time avoiding their pitfalls. This method is based on three pillars.

1. Becoming aware

The first step is to realize that we all use heuristics and are therefore all vulnerable, and that stereotypes influence us even if we do not adhere to them. Even if you see discrimination related to skin color as an aberration, you can still make decisions that are biased by a racial stereotype. A study in the United States, for example, found that participants—whether African American or white—in the role of a police officer, shot unarmed black suspects more often than unarmed white suspects.

2. Motivation to act

The second step is the motivation to act. By accepting that we are easily guided by stereotypes, we become more attentive to social situations that are conducive to heuristics. A little voice in our head tells us: "Be careful! You may have made this decision on the basis of a shortcut. Do you have any other information available? Do you have an objective assessment of the situation?" It becomes clear that we need to put extra effort into asking ourselves these questions and trying to answer them. In the case of recruitment, this may involve reviewing all applications fairly. Simply being aware of our stereotypes will have no effect if we are not motivated to act against them.

3. Provide the necessary cognitive resources

If you are tired, distracted, or short of time, your brain is more likely to use shortcuts than controlled cognition. It is therefore essential to create a suitable working environment when solving a problem or making a decision. In concrete terms, you could put aside an additional time slot to review applications or postpone an important decision until the next morning if you are exhausted after a long working day. It is obvious that time is a scarce commodity for a leader. However, it is worth investing time to reduce the effects of heuristics if the result is of a better quality.

Controlled cognition can successfully reduce the negative impact of heuristics on our decision-making, but it is not the only solution. We can also ensure that we tackle the problem up front in order to eliminate it, or at least reduce its effects. For example, a recruitment process can be rendered anonymous to avoid gender or racial stereotypes, which is what philharmonic orchestras did to reduce discrimination in hiring. They replaced traditional auditions with blind auditions (where the candidate is behind a screen). After this measure was implemented between 1970 and 1980, the rate of women in orchestras rose from 5 percent to 25 percent. Another method to increase diversity within your team, department, or company is the contact hypothesis: the more often you are exposed to diversity, the more open you are to it. However, while this technique works relatively well in reducing the impact of stereotypes, it does not necessarily mean an increase in team performance. Indeed, contrary to what is sometimes implied, diversity is not synonymous with innovation or performance in and of itself. Diversity of employees—often understood in terms of the Benetton advertising style—does not guarantee success. It is not gender, race, or age diversity that enhances the effectiveness and cohesion of a team, it is the variety of skills, functions, and education. It is therefore essential to choose your employees carefully for what they are able to contribute, regardless of any stereotype.

5 Listening Skills

March 27, 1977, Los Rodeos, Tenerife's main airport. Thick fog has drastically reduced visibility, and the arrival of diverted aircraft following a bomb threat at a nearby airport has completely congested Los Rodeos airport. Two airliners, one a KLM and the other a Pan Am, are slowly taxiing along the tarmac, waiting for instructions from the control tower. Because of the total lack of visibility, the control tower and the pilots of both aircraft can only coordinate their movements by radio. The KLM captain understands that he can take off. He begins to accelerate, while the Pan Am aircraft, still on the take-off runway, starts to maneuver. Several messages are exchanged in just a few seconds. Suddenly, the KLM hits the Pan Am aircraft with full force. The death toll is 583.

How could such an accident have occurred? How could this accident, still known as "the crash of the century," have happened, even though the two planes had not yet taken off? The investigation brought together more than seventy international experts, who determined that communication was one of the culprits. As the KLM pilot was about to take off, discussions were taking place between the control tower and the two aircraft on the runway. When questioned by the control tower, the Pan Am pilot replied: "Ok, we'll report when we're clear," indicating that he would confirm when he had left the runway. The KLM pilot incorrectly interpreted this as take-off clearance, despite doubts expressed in the cockpit by the flight engineer. The very marked hierarchy in the cockpit exacerbated communication difficulties between the various parties. The KLM captain failed to listen to the reservations expressed by his flight engineer and began take-off. We know what happened next.

Listening in a Hierarchy

Communicating in a hierarchy poses two main challenges: expressing oneself as a collaborator and listening as a leader. Employees depend on a leader who evaluates their work, sets their objectives, assigns them tasks, and often determines their pay. This dependence can act as a barrier when it comes to transmitting a message, especially if it is a negative one. This is notably the case when (1) the employee encounters a problem that they cannot solve, (2) they want to express an opinion that differs from that of the leader, or (3) they have to pass on negative information to the leader. In the first case, employees are afraid of being perceived as incompetent and of receiving less favorable evaluations. In the second case, they are afraid to question the leader's authority—they may be blamed either way, for remaining silent or for expressing an opposing view. In the third case, employees are reluctant to be the bringer of bad news, announcing, for example, the loss of an important customer. In ancient times, messengers carrying bad news were frequently killed, and although in all probability employees today will not actually be shot because of their message, they nevertheless anticipate their leader's negative reaction and therefore decide, more or less subconsciously, to remain silent or to filter information. They thus unintentionally become accomplices (and often victims) of communication problems related to hierarchies.

As for leaders, listening to the opinions of employees is not always easy, either. They are often afraid of appearing weak or incompetent if they listen too much to the recommendations and criticisms made by employees, especially in the event of a very pronounced hierarchy. Leaders' lack of responsiveness is not limited to employees, it can also affect third parties. To maintain a position of superiority, leaders sometimes ignore valuable expert advice.

These two elements (employees' hesitancy to express themselves and leaders' failure to listen to others) were identified as causes of the Tenerife crash. According to the investigators, the flight engineer hesitated before expressing his doubts and contradicting his superior. The captain decided single-handedly to take off despite opposing information from his crew. This tragedy is far from being an isolated case. Other accidents have occurred for similar reasons. In 1984, a pesticide factory exploded in Bhopal, India, with an official death toll of 7,575 people (however, according to victims' associations, this figure is around 20,000). The investigation revealed that employees had repeatedly sought to draw attention to the plant's safety risks, but were either ignored or punished by their management, who imposed fines or dismissed employees considered too outspoken. In February 2001, another disaster occurred. The American submarine Greenville rose to the surface and hit a Japanese vessel. The result: nine dead. The investigation showed that the fire control technician had identified a ship on his radar but had not dared to report it to his supervisor. His observation contradicted that of the commander who, after a periscope check, cleared the submarine for surfacing.

How to solve these communication problems? In acknowledgment of the findings of the investigation into the Tenerife crash, the aviation sector developed a training program designed to eliminate hierarchical communication deficiencies. Crew Resource Management Training (CRMT) offers concrete measures: employees are encouraged to express themselves and contradict their superiors, and leaders are encouraged to listen and integrate the information provided by their employees. Today, CRMT is taught in many sectors, including hospitals and oil platforms.

Although CRMT is mainly used to deal with crisis situations, it offers solutions to the daily problems experienced by companies. The main objectives are to encourage colleagues to express themselves and to teach leaders to listen. Employees who have a "voice"—who speak up and are listened to—perform better. Creating an organizational climate that is focused on listening is therefore essential.

An Organizational Climate Focused on Listening

To create such a climate, it is first and foremost necessary to reduce the barriers imposed by a rigid hierarchy, for example, by creating physical and temporal spaces that allow employees to express themselves more freely. Weekly or monthly meetings are good practice. By sharing the meeting agendas before the sessions and offering collaborators the opportunity to add discussion points, they are encouraged to speak up and contribute their knowledge and skills. Similarly, a space for voicing one's opinions or concerns can be created through a system of anonymous feedback and suggestions. By protecting the identity of critics, the fear of negative repercussions is reduced.

The rearrangement of offices can also help to improve listening. In particular, physical distance tends to reduce opportunities for communication and, consequently, knowledge transfer and cooperation. Companies with teams spread over several geographical sites are well aware of this problem and employ different strategies to address it. A simple approach is to reduce the distance. In Lausanne, the different teams of the Olympic Committee were spread over two sites, three miles apart. This gap was enough to encourage the construction of a new building, large enough to accommodate the teams from both sites.

A second strategy is to create opportunities for exchange in order to reduce distance. This is the role of the coffee machine. A bank manager in France used to regularly visit branches in the regions for which he was responsible, bringing croissants and *pains au chocolat* (a croissant filled with chocolate, definitely worth trying). By doing so, he created an informal gathering within which his leadership role was less prominent, and collaborators felt freer to speak their minds. Problems that were not transmitted through official channels were often raised around the coffee machine. Yet another strategy is to reduce the physical barriers between superiors and employees. Alcoa, the world's third-largest aluminum producer, has an open space environment with no private offices, not even for senior managers.

These solutions are only suggestions. Other strategies can promote exchange. By creating an environment conducive to listening, the foundations are laid for good communication between employees and leaders.

Employees Who Speak Up

When we talk about communication, there are always two elements: the expresser and the listener. An organizational climate that is focused on listening therefore necessarily requires employees who dare to speak up and who know how to express themselves clearly in front of their superiors. During the Tenerife crash, the co-pilot hesitated to state his position. The same applied to the Greenville submarine: the fire control technician noticed a ship on his radar but did not report it to his supervisor.

For employees to feel comfortable expressing themselves, they must be made aware of their responsibilities as team members and of the importance of the information they hold for decision-making. They must also learn the notions of "false positive" and "false negative." In the case of doubt, it is better to say something, even if you are wrong (raising the alarm for nothing), than to say nothing when you should (not raising the alarm when in fact there is a fire). Generally, such awareness-raising takes the form of workshops during which real cases such as Tenerife and Greenville are studied. Collaborators are invited to reflect on, discuss, and share similar experiences, thus familiarizing themselves with these concepts.

Once the collaborators have been made aware of the need to speak up, they must be trained to communicate clearly. In high-risk environments, such as in a surgical team or an elite intervention unit (SWAT in the United States), members must agree on a specific vocabulary beforehand. Standard terms such as "Hold right" or "Clear left" are used by US military forces to avoid problems of misunderstanding in the event of joint intervention. In companies, abbreviations and technical terms are also used to quickly convey information: "The customer must sign a B-62 form." As in the US military, it is important to clarify what these terms refer to, especially when working with collaborators from different backgrounds. Since each profession has its own vocabulary, the same terms can sometimes describe different things. The leader can help employees to express themselves clearly by defining with them the meaning of certain keywords and clarifying ambiguities.

Once the right listening environment has been created and the employees have been trained to express themselves, the most important part remains: listening. This task is more difficult than it seems, because we retain on average only about 50 percent of what others tell us during a conversation. It is therefore essential that leaders develop their listening skills by mastering the "Triangle of Active Listening."

The Triangle of Active Listening

The "Triangle of Active Listening" consists of three key elements: (1) stimulate, (2) listen, and (3) rephrase.

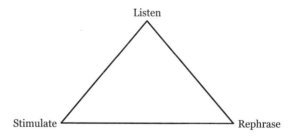

Stimulate

To become a good listener, you need to start off by stimulating your employees and encouraging them to express themselves. To do so, you must give them time and attention. The classic mistake—often mentioned by managers during our in-company training courses—is to squeeze a meeting with an employee in between two important appointments, in order to get it over with as quickly as possible. Sensing this, the employee will find it difficult to share their concerns and thoughts. Another mistake involves a lack of attention and only listening haphazardly, with one's eyes fixed on one's mobile phone. Like a lack of time, a lack of attention is an obstacle to exchange.

Some techniques can help stimulate expression. Open-ended questions, rather than closed-ended questions, promote speaking. Instead of asking employees if they agree with the existing procedure (a yes or no answer), they should be asked what they think about it. They can also be set at ease by telling them that we ourselves do not have an answer to the problem, a more common case than you might think. How can a leader have an answer to everything?

Follow-up questions are another way to encourage an employee to elaborate on a particular topic: "Why do you think this procedure is not practical?" Be careful, however, not to ask for an opinion if you plan to ignore it when making a decision. That's like serving mussels to a customer who ordered steak. Mussels are good, but why ask for an opinion if the decision has already been made?

Stimulation is based on our verbal and nonverbal behavior. Their alignment is essential. Indeed, if we ask an open-ended question, but remain stoic with respect to the answer, look away, or even interrupt the answer, our reactions will be perceived as a lack of interest and will incite the employee to keep quiet. Nonverbal behavior that is indicative of signaling involvement in the exchange comprises smiling, maintaining eye contact, nodding, or communicating interest by taking notes or reacting to the other's words with "I see," "Oh, really!" etc.

Listen

Being able to listen means being able to create a link with the other. A leader's job is to really try and understand their employees by putting aside all preconceptions and keeping an open mind. As we have seen above (Chapter 4), it is important to avoid stereotypes and be wary about heuristics. When the employee commits an error, a leader must, for example, give the employee the benefit of the doubt. As in the judicial system, a suspect remains innocent until proven guilty.

Understanding also implies empathy. By putting oneself in an employee's shoes, a leader can better understand them. How do they feel? Are they comfortable or stressed? Why are they stressed? Decoding the other (Chapter 3) is an essential leadership skill; it allows us to correctly perceive employees and adapt our behavior to their reactions. In the context of active listening, knowing how to identify what stresses an employee will help to put them at ease (by starting the discussion with banalities or by reaffirming our trust in and appreciation of their work). Active listening is therefore not limited to the understanding of the meaning of words, it also implies reading the personality of the other person and decoding their emotions, intentions, convictions, and attitudes—information that may sometimes only be embodied fleetingly, with a hesitation, posture, or look.

Rephrase

The ability to rephrase is also necessary for active listening, where the leader acts as a facilitator and interpreter. The final objective is to correctly understand the other's message. To this end, five reformulation techniques are available: mirror reformulation, echo reformulation, deductive reformulation, clarification reformulation, and summary reformulation.

Mirror reformulation consists of paraphrasing, or repeating in your own words, what your conversation partner has just told you. In an echo reformulation, we repeat a word or a sentence to invite the speaker to clarify its meaning. Deductive reformulation takes up the statement of the speaker and draws a hypothesis from it; its goal is to verify that the message has been correctly interpreted. Clarification reformulation invites the other party to clarify the substance of the uttered thought. Finally, the purpose of the summary reformulation is to ensure that the various key elements of the message have been properly understood.

In the following dialogue, John (a manager) is talking to Alex (a collaborator). Alex is usually motivated by new challenges, but he seems reluctant to engage in a new project.

John: So, what do you think about this new idea?

Alex: I don't really know...

John: You don't really know? (*Echo reformulation*)

Alex: I need some time to think about it.

John: If I understand correctly, you don't seem to be convinced... (*Mirror reformulation*)

Alex: Actually, the idea is very interesting but I'm currently a little underwater....

John: So, your workload is too high at the moment? (*Deductive reformulation*)

Alex: Yes. I'm managing five projects simultaneously, and I don't have an assistant to help me...

John: If you had someone to help you, do you think you could free up time for this new project? (*Reformulation clarification*)

Alex: If I had someone efficient working with me, I could delegate the administrative work and focus on strategy and implementation. I could even take care of two additional projects.

John: Okay. You are underwater right now because you lack resources, but if I was able to get extra budget, which would allow you to recruit a person to help you, would you be interested and could you then spare some time to get involved in this project? (*Reformulation summary*)

Alex: Yes.

Although this conversation is just an illustrative example, it is close to what can be observed in reality. The different reformulation techniques invite our interaction partners to speak and clarify their words. If John had not reformulated Alex's answers as the conversation progressed, he probably would not have discovered that Alex needed help to take on new responsibilities. Alex would likely have rejected the project and John might have erroneously concluded that Alex was not as motivated as he thought he was.

Stimulate, listen, and reformulate constitute the "Triangle of active listening." It creates a virtuous circle in which collaborators feel comfortable expressing themselves more readily and leaders can improve their understanding. This approach may be simple, but it is very effective in facilitating communication between people from different hierarchical levels. As Leonardo da Vinci wrote: "Knowing how to listen is to possess, in addition to one's own, the brains of others." There is no point in being a leader if we do not know how to value the skills of our collaborators and let them speak when they have information that can help our decision-making.

If you want to practice these principles of active listening, you can do the following exercise. Find a partner and sit back to back. Ask them to choose a painting, for example, a Picasso, without showing it to you. Take a pencil and paper and ask them to describe the painting to you. Use the active listening principles to clarify what you hear and try to draw the painting. When you are finished, turn around and compare your drawing with the original painting.

6 Being a Good Leader

In 1913, explorer Ernest Shackleton announced an ambitious goal: to be the first to cross the Antarctic. He raised the equivalent of £60,000 (almost US$8 million today) and began to recruit men for his crew. To do so, he published an ad in a London newspaper for which he received more than 5,000 applications:

> Seeking men for perilous travel.
> Low wages, aggressive cold, long hours
> of darkness. Safe and sound return doubtful.
> Honor and recognition if successful.

The journey began, but as they approached Antarctica, the vessel got caught in ice and all they could do was wait. Ernest Shackleton organized life on board. He maintained the physical and psychological health of his crew by arranging theatre shows, sled dog races, and celebrating national holidays and birthdays. They drifted for ten months until the ice began to tighten its grip, slowly crushing the ship's wooden hull. The vessel eventually began to take on water and sink, so Shackleton gave the order to abandon ship and set up camp on the ice, drastically reducing the crew's chance of survival. Shackleton did not despair.

He held regular discussions with his men in order to anticipate their needs and maintain group cohesion. When the crew carpenter mutinied, Shackleton punished him immediately. When one of his men suffered from the cold, he offered his own gloves, even if it meant exposing himself to frostbite. So far, no one had died, but Shackleton knew that it was only a matter of time. Far from all sea routes, the likelihood of help arriving was almost nonexistent. He chose the strongest crew members, reinforced the rescue boats they had been able to save from the shipwreck, and embarked on a last-chance journey. After several days at sea, the boats reached inhabited areas and help was dispatched to save the crew.

Ernest Shackleton's story is fascinating because it highlights the key role of the leader in the success—in this case, survival—of his team. With his multiple leadership skills, Shackleton made strategic decisions one after the other, acquired and managed the resources necessary for the survival of his men, focused on their individual needs, encouraged them not to give up, and defused conflicts. Although it is rare today to encounter such extreme situations, the role of the leader remains similarly complex.

What Kind of Leader Are You?

Blue. Red. Dominant. Extroverted. There are many ways of classifying leaders. Some are based on scientific evidence, others have more dubious origins. When we talk about leadership styles, we are referring first and foremost to competencies or skills. Skills can be relational, strategic, or technical. Managing a team requires all of them, as well as the ability to apply them at the right time. Here we are focusing on relational or interpersonal skills.

Every leader should master at least four key interpersonal skills: the ability to inspire and motivate colleagues, to develop their skills, to adapt to them. As a source of effective team management, these essential skills will serve as the basis for the upcoming chapters.

1. Inspire your collaborators

Being inspiring is first of all about ensuring that collaborators understand their leader's vision. We are not talking here about economic objectives such as increasing revenue, but rather about a vision of the world that the leader adheres to. IKEA's vision is not to sell as many furniture kits as possible, nor to popularize the Swedish language (or their meatballs), but for people to live "*a better everyday life.*" An effective vision is expressed in a short sentence that gives meaning and moral value to the work of employees. It must express enthusiasm and conviction. Starbucks proposes "*to inspire and nurture the human spirit— one person, one cup and one neighborhood at a time.*" Greenpeace wants to "*ensure the ability of the Earth to nurture life in all its diversity.*" Offering a vision to your employees is not just for top management. It is also an effective tool for middle management, which occupies a privileged position in relation to its staff and customers. It is clear that the vision of a department head will be less abstract than that of an entire company such as IKEA or Starbucks. However, the vision of middle managers can be equally relevant and inspiring, and successfully rally their employees. A customer service manager could aim to be *"the reason for company customers' loyalty."* For a head of HR, it could be *"creating and developing the company's most valuable resource,"* its employees.

However, it is not enough to express a clear vision, it is also necessary to ensure that employees adhere to it. Think of the student revolution in the 1960s. They did not agree with their parents' idea of the world, and instead decided to grow their hair and live life from day to day on a beach, surfing and making love rather than putting on a suit and tie and moving to a residential area in the suburbs. There are several ways to unite your employees around a vision. You can use charismatic communication like Nelson Mandela, Barack Obama, and Charles de Gaulle, or you can set an example—a method adopted by a large number of leaders. As Albert Schweitzer, doctor, philosopher, and theologian, honored with the Nobel Peace Prize, said: "The example is not the main thing that influences others. It's the only thing." If you want your employees to treat their colleagues and customers with respect, you must treat them with respect. If you want them to volunteer for certain tasks that require considerable effort and investment, you must be the first to get your hands dirty. Like Shackleton who gave his gloves to one of his sailors, a leader must demonstrate to team members that it is only by working together that they can succeed (or survive the shipwreck, in the case of Shackleton).

2. Motivate your collaborators

To inspire is to set a direction. Motivating your employees means giving yourself the means to advance in the set direction. The first motivational tool is goal setting. Goals will translate your vision into a succession of steps that are achievable and thus motivating. Whether it is a question of personal or professional goals, we suggest you favor so-called "SMART" goals.

A SMART goal is *specific*, one that is clear, precise, and unambiguous. It must then be *measurable*, that is, it must be possible to measure performance and objectively establish whether the goal was achieved. It must also be *ambitious* to stimulate employees, while remaining *realistic*, and therefore attainable, so as not to discourage them. Finally, it must be *temporally* defined with a fixed duration or deadline. For an after-sales manager, a SMART objective could be to achieve 80 percent customer satisfaction by the end of the year. Given that customer satisfaction in the previous quarter was 75 percent, the target would respond to all five SMART parameters.

Another motivational tool is the carrot and stick— reward and punishment. On the one hand, a bonus or promotion if goals are achieved; on the other hand, blame, suspension, or even dismissal when not. These systems are usually predictable, predefined, and dependent on employee performance. However, even if rewards and punishments are effective leadership tools—particularly to increase employee satisfaction and motivation—it is important to keep in mind that the role of the leader is also to show recognition.

Recognition—expressing appreciation for a task accomplished and well done—is a leadership tool that is too often underused. During our training sessions, managers often mention this shortcoming. Some even fear that they will lose credibility or demotivate their collaborators by showing them their appreciation. However, recognizing the successes and efforts of team members is as important as giving them feedback on their poor performance. This is all the more true since simple verbal recognition can increase motivation and well-being at work, while its absence may negatively affect the quality of the relationship between leaders and their employees. A senior manager once reported the following example. Several months after the engagement of a new secretary, whose work was of excellent quality, the secretary asked her if there was something wrong or whether the senior manager was not satisfied with her work. The senior manager was surprised by the question and after discussing with the secretary about her reasons for asking the question, understood that her apparently too concise and direct e-mails were the origin. She immediately reassured the secretary that she was extremely satisfied, which is why she did not further develop her messages. However, not saying anything leaves a space for employees to (mis)interpret the most innocuous elements in their own way (such as the blunt and factual tone of an e-mail). By forgetting to acknowledge the quality of her secretary's work, the senior manager had failed in her role as a motivator.

3. Developing your collaborators' skills

Good leaders not only encourage their employees to do what they want them to do, they also make sure that the collaborators surpass themselves by giving them the opportunity to develop personally within their jobs. Feedback plays an essential role in this respect. Just as it is impossible for a young child to learn to write without feedback from adults, it is difficult to develop professional skills without feedback. Feedback enables respective perceptions to be compared and highlights discrepancies. Identifying a gap opens the door to personal development. In the professional world, giving feedback is mainly the responsibility of the leader. Whether positive or negative, it allows employees to become aware of their strengths and weaknesses and to improve. All leaders must therefore provide feedback. And, it is not just a matter of conducting an appraisal interview once a year, you should get into the habit of giving frequent and regular feedback. We will further develop this powerful leadership tool in Chapter 11.

4. Adapt to your collaborators

Employees must perform the work necessary to accomplish the tasks described in their job descriptions. However, limiting collaborators to this list amounts to seeing them as machines, much like Charlie Chaplin in his film *Modern Times*. Yet, each co-worker has their own personality, a certain working style and communication preference, as well as a set of personal convictions and beliefs. While it is important to treat employees fairly and avoid favoritism, it is also important to take into account their individual differences. This means adapting your behavior to the needs of each individual. For example, if a person works effectively independently, it will be counterproductive to give too many detailed instructions. Excessive guidance will be interpreted as a lack of confidence and will lead to demotivation. Conversely, some people will need clear instructions and a rigorous framework. Leaving them on their own can reduce their performance and motivation. We have been able to demonstrate this in the laboratory: when a leader adapts their leadership style to the different needs of the employees, leaders are perceived more positively. It is therefore necessary for a leader to understand their employees, and particularly to identify their needs, expectations, and preferences in order to adjust to them. Decoding others accurately takes on its full range of meaning here.

The Leadership Toolbox

Like Shackleton, a leader must possess these four key skills to successfully manage employees and use them wisely. Just as a saw is not the right tool to drive in a nail, leaders must know when and how to use their tools. The four skills often overlap but are still geared to particular situations. Inspiring employees will be crucial during a presentation at the beginning of the year, while feedback will be the key element of an end-of-year evaluation. In the following chapters, we will discuss how leaders can use their toolbox according to the challenges they face on a daily basis: public presentations, weekly meetings, negotiation, conflict resolution, or feedback sessions.

EVALUATE YOURSELF

The questionnaire below will allow you to self-assess the four key skills described in this chapter. Answer the eight questions as spontaneously and honestly as possible. You're the only one who will see the result, so give it a go!

To what extent do you agree with the following statements about yourself?

In the work context, I...	Completely disagree (1)	Disagree somewhat (2)	Neither agree nor disagree (3)	Agree somewhat (4)	Completely agree (5)
1. ...behave in a way that takes the needs of others into account.	❑ 1	❑ 2	❑ 3	❑ 4	❑ 5
2. ...impose the same requirements on myself as on my employees.	❑ 1	❑ 2	❑ 3	❑ 4	❑ 5
3. ...set goals for my collaborators.	❑ 1	❑ 2	❑ 3	❑ 4	❑ 5
4. ...provide regular feedback to employees.	❑ 1	❑ 2	❑ 3	❑ 4	❑ 5
5. ...communicate the company's vision with enthusiasm.	❑ 1	❑ 2	❑ 3	❑ 4	❑ 5
6. ...recognize collaborators' achievements.	❑ 1	❑ 2	❑ 3	❑ 4	❑ 5
7. ...do not hesitate to comment on employee performance.	❑ 1	❑ 2	❑ 3	❑ 4	❑ 5
8. ...behave in a way that takes into account the feelings of others.	❑ 1	❑ 2	❑ 3	❑ 4	❑ 5

Work out the average scores obtained for each of the four skills. After calculating your scores[2] for each skill, place them on the diagram below to identify your strengths and weaknesses.

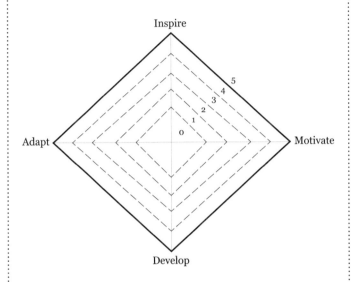

7 How to Give a Killer Presentation

Lucas has sweaty hands and a dry mouth. He has just taken his place at the lectern to present the project he has been working on with his team for several months: new accounting software. He can already see his colleagues' heads hovering over their phones to check on the sports results or answer e-mails. Lucas starts his presentation. He describes the technical details of the software, its advantages and disadvantages. He emphasizes the extra workload that the new software will temporarily impose on his employees. Then he notices that Michael in the third row has fallen asleep. He speeds up and clings to the lectern to calm down. He loses his place and stutters a few times before closing with a joke about his last slide. A few people laugh and Lucas takes his seat again, happy and relieved that the ordeal is finally over.

Emma smiles. She likes to talk in public and convince prospective clients. Today, she is presenting new potential customers with an offer for conducting a risk study. Her clients listen attentively while sitting around a conference table. Some nod occasionally while others take notes. Emma takes advantage of a slide change to move around and occupy the space. She talks without looking at her notes and sometimes pauses. Time flies by. After she concludes, one of the potential clients thanks her. He makes a comment to the effect that she is "charming," but then finishes by saying that the idea of hiring outside consultants to analyze the company's risks is out of the question. Emma reflects and chooses to politely respond that no one likes to go to the proctologist for a rectal exam, but that it's worth it when the doctor detects a cancer. The client turns white and his colleagues smile. The deal is in the bag.

These two examples illustrate the types of presentations we are likely to see. Some, like the one by Lucas, are monotonous and fail to convey a message effectively, while others, like the one by Emma, are inspiring and persuasive. But what is the difference between a good presentation and a bad one? Can we learn to become better public speakers?

The Orator's Pyramid

On January 9, 2007, Steve Jobs addressed an audience of geeks, journalists, and influencers. His presentation was about to transform the mobile phone market—and the world—by unveiling the very first iPhone. Steve Jobs' speech respects what we call the orator's pyramid: an effective structure that includes charismatic verbal and nonverbal behavior.

THE ORATOR'S PYRAMID

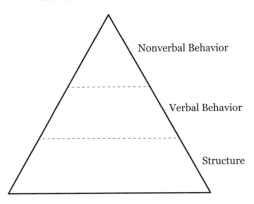

The foundation of a successful presentation is its structure, meaning the choice and quality of the arguments presented, as well as the order in which they are addressed. The second element is charismatic verbal behavior. It refers mainly to words and rhetorical tools, such as metaphors used to illustrate elements of the speech. Finally, nonverbal charismatic behavior supports words and structures with appropriate gestures. Steve Jobs engaged his audience by announcing the three key features of the iPhone before unveiling the product and its benefits. Throughout his speech, he used charismatic verbal tactics, including rhetorical questions and metaphors. He also took to the stage, moving around and modulating his voice to be more engaging.

The reason we use the term "pyramid" rather than "triangle" is because the hierarchy among the elements is important. A leader using his hands perfectly and speaking dynamically will not be able to convey their message effectively if the words are not well chosen. Similarly, excellent verbal and nonverbal behavior within a loose and unorganized structure will make the leader seem serious and competent, but unclear. It is therefore at the foundation level that a good presentation begins—with the structure.

Learn to Walk before You Run

One of the first references to the structure of a discourse goes back to Aristotle. This Greek philosopher suggested breaking it down into three parts: the beginning, middle, and end. The purpose of the beginning is to attract the audience's attention, to establish the credibility of the speaker, and to present the content of the speech in a few words, together with the reasons why the speech should be heard. The middle constitutes the body of the presentation. It is the moment when arguments and ideas are presented to inform or convince the listener. The end summarizes the key points of the speech and concludes with a "call to action." Aristotle could have described this structure more simply: tell your audience what you are going to talk about, talk about it, and then remind them of what you have just talked about.

From a cognitive point of view, this structure makes sense. A listener is subject to primacy and recency effects, meaning that a person retains information given at the beginning and at the end of a conversation particularly well. Summarizing the essentials at the beginning and at the end of a speech or presentation is therefore crucial.

Does this mean that all presentations must follow the same structure? Of course not. Every speech is unique and thus different. It is essential to adapt the construction according to its purpose, context, and audience. Like a tailor, you need to understand your clients' tastes and expectations in order to suggest a cut and fabric. Who are they? How many of them are there? Why are they here? What language do they speak? Depending on the answers to each of these questions, the speech will be structured differently. Emma and Lucas face radically different audiences. Emma is in a small conference room with a dozen people who understand the jargon she uses and who are listening to her so that they can decide whether or not to sign a contract with her company. Her goal is to convince them to accept her offer. As for Lucas, he is talking to a group of about thirty employees from various departments of his firm. They are not familiar with technical terms or specific problems related to accounting. Moreover, he is not trying to convince but to inform them about the changes they will have to adapt to. It is therefore only after answering the above questions that you can begin to develop a presentation strategy around one or several key messages.

As we have seen previously (Chapter 4), the cognitive capacities of our brains are limited. We can only record and process a certain amount of information.

We must therefore consider our audience as a container—smaller rather than larger—capable of accommodating only a restricted number of key messages. In practice, this means focusing on the most important messages so that the audience can remember them. To identify them, here is a tip we often give: imagine what you would like a listener to take away from the presentation. What would that person say to someone who could not attend but is interested in knowing what was said in the presentation? You should write down these key messages on a piece of paper and keep them within easy reach during the preparation of your speech.

"Ready-to-Wear" Structures

The purpose, audience, and context are clear, and you have identified your key messages. Now it is time to build the structure of your presentation. There is one important rule to follow: each argument, idea, or slide should logically lead to the following. At no time should the listener wonder where you are going and how you will get there. If you follow this rule, you are free to build a unique structure or to use one of the many "ready-to-wear" models. Here are three examples.

The "problem-solution" structure is used to persuade or sell. You start by presenting the problem, follow up with the proposed solution and its benefits, and then conclude with a call to action. If you wanted to sell earmuffs, it would go something like this: "Are you tired of your hair getting tousled every time you put on a hat?

With earmuffs, no more rebellious hair! Your ears stay warm and your hairstyle intact. So, what are you waiting for? Discover our products on earmuffs.com."

The structure of the "problem-residue" model also aims to convince, but this time in the context of an opposition. The presenter begins by announcing the problem, then outlines the opponents' solutions and their limits. Then comes the "best" solution with its advantages, and finally, as in the case of the "problem-solution" structure, a call to action. Let's imagine the same earmuff salesperson speaking at an annual headband sales convention. His speech could be structured as follows: "Are you tired of tousled hair every time you put on a hat? Most people in this room will tell you that you need a headband. What they won't tell you is that headbands are just as messy as hats. However, if you wear earmuffs, no more rebellious hair! Your ears stay warm, your head cool, and your hairstyle intact. So, don't hesitate! Come and discover our products on earmuffs.com."

The third and final structure we will focus on is demonstration. Its purpose is to present the particularities of a product by "demonstrating" its results. We start with the "why": why is this product useful? Then we present the product's attractiveness or results, before concluding with a summary of the key elements. For example, the presentation of the earmuffs could be structured as follows: "Why is it essential that we discuss the third-quarter sales figures? As you know, we are about to enter the most important period of the year for the sale of earmuffs. Just like a football team needs to know what went well and not so well in their last game, I think it's fundamental to understand why some products sold well and others flopped. There are three key figures that I would like to present to you today. ... In conclusion, remember these two key points: sell black to your distributors and cut your prices by 5 percent."

You have to take your time choosing and adapting the structure of your speech according to your objectives and the circumstances of the presentation. Once the structure has become clear, you can begin to work on your verbal behavior.

Talking like Martin Luther King or Winston Churchill

When people are asked to think of charismatic leaders, some names come up repeatedly: Martin Luther King, Winston Churchill, Michelle Obama, Margaret Thatcher, Nelson Mandela, or Steve Jobs. Whether political figures or CEOs, these leaders were able to inspire and convince by the force of their speeches. In addition to being brilliantly structured, their communication styles exploit certain verbal tactics to persuade and inspire their listeners. Researchers have identified the tactics that many of these speakers use, making them charismatic, influential, and inspiring. Here they are.

1. Stories

The first tactic involves the use of storytelling, as in this example of a speech by Barack Obama in 2013 on the Affordable Care Act: "I remember the fear Michelle and I felt when Sasha was a few months old and she got meningitis. And we raced to the hospital and they had to give her a spinal tap. And we didn't know what was wrong and we were terrified, never felt so scared or helpless in all of my life. But we were fortunate enough to have good health insurance. And I remember looking around that emergency room and thinking—what about the parents who aren't that lucky?" Stories work. They make it easier to understand and remember a message. They typically evoke emotions as the audience identifies with the characters. Ideally, a story should be short, simple, and powerful. Most stories follow the following sequence: a character encounters a difficulty or a problem and struggles to find a solution allowing them to emerge from the challenge and find themselves in a better place than at the outset of the story. You could, for example, describe the evolution of a project as follows: "This project was born the day James, who was looking for a graphic designer, couldn't find a website comparing the offers and prices of graphic designers in the region (difficulty). First, we spent months trying to convince our superiors to invest in our project and the development was not without difficulties. We almost lost all our data the day a hacker pirated our website (struggle to find a solution). But finally, after a year and a half of work and relentless effort, we are very happy to present our platform that enables users to find the ideal graphic designer in one click (the solution is in place and people are better off than at the outset)."

2. Metaphors

Like stories, metaphors make it easier to understand and remember a message. In our introductory case, Emma uses a metaphor successfully. She compares her job to that of a doctor and risk audits to an unpleasant medical procedure that can save lives. In contrast, Lucas does not use any metaphors and fails to spark the interest of his colleagues. He could easily have compared the current accounting system to a faulty washing machine that needed replacement. The field of metaphorical possibilities is infinite. However, certain comparisons are often used in the business world, such as those relating to war, medicine, or sports.

3. Contrasts

Contrasts are stylistic figures that oppose a rejected argument or idea to the argument or idea being defended. Probably one of the most well-known examples is that of John Fitzgerald Kennedy: "Don't ask what your country can do for you; ask what you can do for your country." In most charismatic narratives, the contrasts follow the same pattern: "It's not [an argument or an idea that is rejected], it's [an argument or idea that is promoted]."

4. Three-part list

Three-part lists can be either explicit or implicit. An explicit list would be, for example: "So far we have dealt with three tactics: first, stories, second, metaphors, and third, contrasts." While an implicit list would be: "So far we have dealt with stories, metaphors, and contrasts." Three-part lists allow you to structure an argument or even a speech as well as focusing attention on a few, easily memorized elements. Why three? There is no scientific answer to this question, but it seems that the number three gives a feeling of comprehensiveness, while at the same time containing strong symbolism (think of the Trinity, the Three Musketeers, or the Three Little Pigs, for example).

5. Repetitions

The phrase "I have a dream" that Martin Luther King repeated several times in his 1963 speech is a canonical example of this rhetorical figure. Repetition works differently from lists, because it is used primarily for style and to support an argument. For repetition to be effective, the syntax needs to be repeated in the same way when introducing a series of elements, for example: "Where were you when our competitors attacked us personally? Where were you when our customers asked us for explanations?"

6. Rhetorical questions

Rhetorical questions are questions that do not require an answer, or more precisely, questions that contain the answer in themselves. They can be used to stimulate the minds of the listeners or to direct their attention to the issue at hand. After his dismissal from Apple, Steve Jobs asked the rhetorical question in one of his speeches: "How can you get fired from the company you started?"

7. *Express moral conviction*

In order to speak of moral conviction, the words you use must meet two criteria: express what you believe or don't believe (convictions) and state your values (morals). For example: "Racism is intolerable, regardless of the context, the people involved, or the reasons given." In the everyday life of a company, stating moral convictions may seem both abstract and inappropriate, but there are many opportunities if we broaden our range of values. When Lucas presented his new accounting system, for example, he could have emphasized the value of teamwork: "No one should have to shoulder the burden of such a project alone. We all have to shoulder the burden together."

8. *Express what the group is feeling*

By expressing what the group is feeling, we are demonstrating to those listening that we understand how they feel. As a leader, we want to be able to reduce the distance between ourselves and the audience, not physically (there are sixty inches between us and the audience, for example) but psychologically (even if we are sitting next to them, the CEO of Nestlé will seem more distant to us than the owner of a SME). Shortly after the San Bernardino shooting in the United States, Barack Obama decided to adopt the stance of a father rather than that of a president. His goal was to put himself on the same level as his fellow citizens: "As a father to two young daughters who are the most precious part of my life, I know that we see ourselves with friends and coworkers at a holiday party like the one in San Bernardino..."

9. Set ambitious goals

As we saw in the section on structure, most speeches end with a call to action. It is therefore not surprising that great speakers regularly set ambitious goals for their audiences. In 1962, John Fitzgerald Kennedy set probably one of the most ambitious goals of his career when he addressed an audience at Rice University in Texas: "We choose to go to the moon in this decade." Seven years later, the goal was achieved.

10. Create confidence that goals can be achieved

Closely related to the previous tactic, this one aims to reassure employees by communicating that the objectives set, although ambitious, will be achieved or at least are achievable. A simple sentence such as "I'm convinced that we'll get there" can be enough to instill a sense of confidence.

Preparing Your Presentation

The tactics we have just described do not solely belong to great orators. They can be learned and used in everyday life, both in presentations and in informal discussions. During our training courses, we advise managers to begin by writing a speech that they intend to give and then to work on it, first in writing, trying to apply the tactics that they consider sensible and useful. Here, quality takes priority over quantity. One very good metaphor is better than three weaker ones. In addition, several tactics can be combined in one sentence, for example, a three-part list and a contrast. When you are ready, meaning that your presentation is well structured and you have incorporated several tactics into your notes, it is time to address the top of the pyramid, nonverbal behavior.

Nonverbal Behavior

One of the reasons for getting stressed when we give a presentation is the impression that the listeners will notice our every movement and will focus on any uncertain gesture. This is obviously an illusion. What is true, however, is that nonverbal behavior can make a presentation more engaging and allow us to grab the audience's attention.

Let's first consider the voice. We've all had a teacher whose monotonous voice only encouraged our desire to drop off to sleep after lunch. When we communicate, we have to aim for dynamism. It's not a matter of shouting or getting over-excited, but rather of varying your speaking speed, modulating the volume and tone of your voice, and allowing a moment of silence to accentuate a point or to retain listeners' attention.

Next comes the use of arms and hands. In general, displaying an open posture is recommended. You can emphasize some of your words with your hands, for example by pointing to number three while illustrating a three-part list, or you can accentuate variations in the tone of your voice with small gestures. The former French president, Nicolas Sarkozy, was particularly fond of these rhythmic gestures.

The third element is the gaze. Eye contact ensures that those listening continue to pay attention and creates a connection between us and the audience. It helps us to convey information, but also allows us to receive valuable feedback from the audience so that we can provide the necessary clarifications if needed. When several people frown over a technical or complicated issue, it will signal to us that the message may not have been understood and that we may need to tackle the explanation from a different angle.

The fourth and final element is moving around. While concentrating on a speech, the speaker may tend to remain static. If, like Emma, we are in a small meeting room, this is not a problem. In a large room, however, moving around can be essential to hold the audience's attention.

This list is obviously not exhaustive, far from it. However, it is complete enough to give you the keys to a good presentation. Mastering each of these nonverbal behaviors takes time and experience, and each individual has their own specific behaviors to focus on. It is not a question of putting everyone in the same mold, but of awakening the individuality and authenticity of each person. Respecting a systematic order in the preparation of your speech (structure, verbal and non-verbal behavior) will make it easier to develop natural, personalized gestures. Indeed, the verbal elements of a speech (metaphors, stories, three-part lists, rhetorical questions, etc.) will naturally inspire gestures and modulations in your voice.

Don't hesitate to experiment at home, or in a real-life situation to find out which behaviors suit you and which seem adequate, spontaneous, or unnatural. The difficulty is in finding the right balance between authenticity and originality. Although the goal is to reinforce your charisma and strengthen your message, never lose sight of the fact that you should feel comfortable with your gestures and how you behave nonverbally.

Manage Your Stress

Public speaking is a stressful exercise. As always, good preparation can considerably reduce the level of anxiety. Breathing techniques can be helpful, or you can make sure that you go first to avoid prolonging the waiting period. We tested another solution in the laboratory: thinking about a past situation in which you felt powerful. You can think back, for example, to a sporting victory or a brilliant speech you delivered in front of a small audience. This remembered sense of power helps to reduce stress and thus improve your performance.

Showtime

Today, speeches are part of the job description for many leaders. Whether it is to present your business's financial results, convince clients, or inform employees, leaders must know how to speak in public. In our experience, the advice in this chapter is equally useful to both novices and experienced people, even in cases where public speaking is not a particularly appreciated task.

TIME TO PRACTICE!

The best way to improve your public speaking skills is to practice. To do so, prepare a short speech that will be useful in your professional life, such as a brief presentation of your company or department, or an end-of-year toast, following the steps discussed above.

Start by working on the structure and write down your key messages on a piece of paper. Then, draw an outline of your speech.

When you are satisfied with the structure, move on to verbal tactics. Try several techniques and combinations.

Rack your brain to find the right metaphor or story to convey your message. Read your speech aloud and ask yourself how you would react to hearing it from someone else. What is good? What is missing? What is too much?

Finally, work on your nonverbal behavior. Think about a few gestures that are suited to your verbal techniques and start practicing. Repeat your speech several times until you no longer need your notes. When you are ready, film yourself. Use the video to see which behaviors need to be removed or modified. Then start again until you get the desired result. With experience, you will need less and less time to prepare.

8   How to Organize an Effective Meeting

It's 8:30 a.m. in the office of an SME that produces cookies for the mass market. Members of the marketing, human resources, and production departments have gathered together to discuss a new project: a line of savory cookies. Julia is heading the team; she is the one who called the meeting. She has set aside enough time for her co-workers to discuss the project and has reserved the Matterhorn meeting room, the one with the large rectangular table. The first collaborator to arrive is Richard. He's the "loudmouth" of the company. He sits down at the end of the table and starts to talk about his weekend. Richard is the exact opposite to Liam, a creative but discreet young man, who settles down with his computer near the door. The other employees arrive one after the other; ten minutes after the scheduled time, the meeting finally begins when Julia interrupts the people chatting and starts the group brainstorming activity. Ideas soon start to flow, but the discussion is quickly monopolized by just a few employees. The subject deviates several times. Two hours go by, and the discussions get bogged down. At 11.30 a.m., Julia ends the meeting. She goes back to her desk and flops into her chair, wondering why on earth the meeting was so unproductive.

As Diverse as It Gets

Meetings are an important part of every leader's agenda. A study conducted in the United States reports the impressive figure of eleven million meetings per day. In large companies, a manager spends about 75 percent of his time in meetings, which is almost eight times more than in small companies.

Despite (or perhaps because of) their importance in the life of the company, meetings are often identified as a time-consuming and unproductive event. Some surveys even go so far as to point out that 50 percent of time spent in meetings is unnecessarily wasted. Are all meetings therefore inefficient and expensive? No. However, these figures underline how important it is for a manager to know when to schedule a meeting and how to run it.

In general, a meeting has one of the following six objectives: sharing information, training collaborators, brainstorming, solving a problem, making decisions, or socializing. Obviously, the character of the meeting will vary according to these objectives. A training course will not involve as much interaction from collaborators as a brainstorming session. Likewise, summarizing second quarter results will not take as long as an in-depth review of the accounts over the same period. Despite the fact that there are many types of meetings, good practice can enable us to maximize efficiency and increase satisfaction for collaborators involved in all kinds of meetings.

What Is the Goal?

A meeting is successful only if it achieves an established objective. If there is no clear goal to achieve, it is difficult to know whether the meeting was successful. In the case of her brainstorming, Julia wanted to initiate a new project, but she did not set any specific goals. Her collaborators suggested ideas and discussed the pros and cons but ended the session without a sense of accomplishment. Like Julia, many professionals mention this same feeling of discouragement when asked about meetings and how effective they perceive them to be.

It is therefore essential to set clear goals before any meeting. These should ideally be SMART (see Chapter 6) in order to motivate staff, but also to give the leader the opportunity to steer the various interventions in the same direction and thus facilitate cooperation within the group, especially when stakeholders have divergent interests. These goals can be communicated verbally during the meeting or in writing prior to the meeting via, for example, an agenda. In the case of Julia, three departments were present. They all have different annual objectives, constraints, and concerns. By setting a specific objective (such as the development of a short list of five savory concepts that meet the company's production and distribution constraints), Julia could have facilitated discussions between the departments by forcing them to work together to achieve the goal. Moreover, she could have communicated this objective before the meeting so that the different departments could have come prepared. Finally, she could have concluded the session as soon as the goal was reached, giving the participants a strong sense of accomplishment and additional motivation.

Who Should Be There and Why?

Imagine yourself for a moment in the following position: you are part of the human resources department and Julia comes into your office to invite you to a brainstorming session about creating new savory cookies. During the meeting, you find yourself sitting between people from marketing and production, and you have no clue as to what they are talking about. Their jargon-filled discussion goes on and on, and you soon start to regret having left your phone on your desk; you could have at least passed the time playing Candy Crush. Afterwards, you go back to your desk, mourning those two wasted hours in a meeting that had nothing to do with you.

A meeting is a difficult exercise in cooperation; several people sit in an enclosed space (often a meeting room with the name of a mountain, a town, or a famous person), trying to communicate effectively with each other. The difficulty of the exercise increases with the number of participants. With three people (and therefore three different personalities) around a table, the challenge is easily mastered, especially if one of the three collaborators is a manager. For a one-hour meeting, assuming a fair distribution of speaking time, each of the three people would have twenty minutes. Moreover, the stakes are limited, as such a meeting represents a cumulative human cost of only three hours for the company. With six people, the exercise becomes more complicated. Speaking times melt like snow in the sun, personalities multiply, and the hourly cost doubles. With ten people, the average speaking time drops to six minutes (not counting the time it takes to coordinate the ten personalities), for a total cumulative human cost of ten hours. As a leader, you must therefore ensure that the presence of each person can be justified. Coordination becomes more complex and the cost of the meeting dramatically increases as more people become involved.

There is a twofold goal. First, you want your employees to adequately prepare before the meeting starts, and second, you want them to actively participate in the meeting. As we saw earlier, a leader must be able to motivate and give meaning to the actions of collaborators, in this case by explaining the "why" of their presence. Knowing that one's work has a purpose is an essential motivating factor. In an experiment conducted by economist Dan Ariely, who is well known for his TED talks, participants were paid $3 for each Bionicle Lego figure they built and were free to build as many as they wanted. For some participants, Dan

Ariely and his colleagues gave sense to their actions by closely observing each constructed figure, taking notes, and carefully storing it in a box. For other participants, the figures were destroyed as soon as they were built, and the participants made their next figure with the same pieces. Those who constructed without purpose, built 57 percent fewer figures than those who felt that their work was useful. In the same way, every collaborator needs to understand why they are participating in a meeting and why their involvement is important. The question "What am I doing here?" should never cross their minds.

In Which Environment Should the Meeting Take Place?

It's Thursday night and you're going out with your team members to celebrate a birthday. When you walk into the bar, you have two options. On the right, a coffee table and comfortable armchairs at fairly wide distances from each other; on the left, a high table surrounded by tall stools. You will probably choose the high table because you know that the space between the armchairs will be detrimental to a conversation involving the whole team. The stools will allow for movement and therefore opportunities to interact with several people.

This example underlines how we instinctively read our environment—meaning the physical and sensory elements that surround us—to understand the effects it will have on our behavior, especially in a context of social interaction. During a meeting, the environment includes furniture and its layout, as well as light, noise, and temperature. As a leader, there is no need to become a Feng Shui master, but it can be useful to think of some basic rules that can improve or hinder the dynamics of a meeting.

First of all, the furniture, especially the table. Julia had reserved a room with a rectangular table and let Richard sit at the head. She hadn't considered how this strategic position allows the person sitting there to see everyone. The head of the table is also frequently associated with the hierarchically dominant person. By giving this position to Richard, who is known for being extraverted and talkative, the dynamics of the meeting were undoubtedly affected, as it encouraged him to speak more than was fair. If Julia had asked Richard to choose another seat or had booked a round table, she would probably have gotten more out of the shy Liam.

Another important element is external factors: a neon light that flashes like a disco ball, a worker jackhammering the pavement, a room that is too cold or too hot... All these elements affect the concentration and active participation of employees. It is not always possible to control everything, but mastering a few details can make all the difference between the failure and success of a meeting. We once witnessed a meeting of thirty bankers called by their director to inform them of the bank's future. After six months of rumors, nerves were frayed. As the director walked into the room, he noticed the temperature was far too high. He postponed the session for twenty minutes and then moved everyone to a smaller but cooler room. When he announced the takeover by a competitor, a few employees were upset, of course, but no one got angry. This manager had just shown sensitivity in understanding that aggression increases with temperature, a reality proven by research.

How to Manage Time

When organizing a meeting, time should be approached in two ways: as a resource to be consumed and as a resource to be allocated strategically. In the first case, try to minimize the length of the meeting by making sure you start on time, keeping an eye on the clock, and, if necessary, reminding participants of the session's objectives. In the second case, make an effort to distribute floor time intelligently so that all key information is shared.

Julia had remained relatively passive during the exchanges in her meeting. She listened and offered her point of view, but almost never interrupted her colleagues, even when they strayed from the subject. Similarly, she did not try to allocate floor time. The result? People like Liam were not given the opportunity to share potentially crucial information. The leader must therefore play the dual role of facilitator and time master, monitoring the discussion by encouraging speaking and listening, while at the same time making sure that the goals are achieved within the allotted time.

How to Deal with Individual Differences?

The last aspect concerns managing individual differences. A meeting is a collection of personalities, knowledge, and skills. Just as a bartender needs to know how to mix ingredients to make a balanced and delicious cocktail, a leader needs to leverage individual differences to ensure a successful meeting.

The leader's challenge is to adapt, as we saw in Chapter 6, to the needs and expectations of his collaborators. In the context of a meeting, this may, for example, involve adjusting vocabulary, especially if the session brings together people from different departments. Technical words and acronyms may not only impair understanding and the exchange of information, but their use can also create a feeling of being left out. Behavior sometimes needs to be adapted as well. In Julia's case, Richard (the "loudmouth" of the team) needed to be restrained to make room for his colleagues, while Liam (a shy fellow) needed to be encouraged to speak up. Adapting not only makes for a more productive meeting, but also increases employee satisfaction.

A Multifaceted Tool

Meetings don't have to be the pet peeve of collaborators. On the contrary, by adopting a few good practices, they become an extremely efficient tool for making decisions, exchanging information, or solving problems. It goes without saying that certain rules must be adapted to the context and objective of the meeting. For example, video conferencing poses altogether new challenges for the leader. Problems with lighting and furniture are replaced by problems with network connection, camera framing, or microphones. Other issues, however, remain the same. It is still essential that those present in a video conference have a valid reason for attending the meeting. Similarly, it is always necessary to set goals and manage time. Thus, although meetings are all different, the quality of a meeting can be improved by following a few simple guidelines, as outlined below.

CHECKLIST FOR A SUCCESSFUL MEETING
- Are the objectives clearly defined and communicated to participants?
- Do all participants have a valid reason for attending?
- Does the environment favor concentration and exchange?
- Is it possible to reduce the time required without compromising the objectives?

9 How to Manage Conflicts

A Lesson in Diplomacy

Although everything seems to be going well in your team, for the past few weeks you've been hearing through the grapevine about tension between two of your team members, Alexander and Mia. Since you haven't noticed anything out of the ordinary yourself, and they still seem to be getting along well, you have not taken these rumors seriously and have not intervened. However, today, in the middle of the weekly meeting, Mia confronted Alexander in front of the whole team. She accused him of responding too slowly to internal e-mails, thus interfering with the team's communication process, and criticized him for making no effort to adapt to new technologies. In response to the accusations, Alexander got carried away and replied to Mia that he wasn't going to be told how to do his job by a "young punk." Given the situation, you decided to postpone the rest of the meeting and asked Alexander and Mia to come to your office to clear the air and find a solution to their conflict.

How would you handle this meeting with these two collaborators who do not seem to be able to get along with each other anymore? What would you do to solve the conflict? The purpose of this chapter is to propose answers to such questions.

Interpersonal conflicts are frequent in companies. For example, a survey showed that out of 1,200 work interactions sampled, 22.5 percent of them were described as conflictual by workers. Conflicts are therefore part of the daily life of leaders and can have negative repercussions on the company as a whole, if not resolved quickly and efficiently. Just as a doctor must know the symptoms of an illness and its development, a leader must understand the origins and impact of conflict, as well as the conflict process itself, in order to be able to contain it.

Conflicts in the Workplace

Where do conflicts come from? Three elements suffice to bring them out. First, the perception of a threat to someone's interests, needs, or values. Second, an interdependence between the people involved, where the actions of one impact those of the other. Third, a sense of intentional harm or harmful neglect. These three elements are found in the example of Alexander and Mia. Mia finds that Alexander takes too long to respond to e-mails (threat), which prevents her from moving forward in her work (interdependence). In addition, she does not see any effort from Alexander to change his behavior even after having explained to him how problematic it is for her (neglect).

These three key elements of conflict also explain why conflicts are so frequent in the workplace. Feeling that one's interests are being threatened is common in business since financial, time, and human resources are as necessary to achieving an objective (respecting a deadline or a budget, for example) as they are limited. Imagine yourself in charge of a project that is vital to the company. Your success will necessarily depend on meeting deadlines. Two days before the deadline, a collaborator announces that he can no longer invest in your project because he has to submit a report himself. You will probably feel your interests threatened—the first spark of a possible conflict. Moreover, your success here depends on the work of this collaborator. Because the interdependence is very strong, the threat is exacerbated. Ultimately, if you feel like your colleague is trying to harm you or is not taking into account the effect his behavior is having on you, the triad is complete. However, if you were to learn that upper management had imposed a 24-hour deadline for your colleague's report, you would understand that his not investing in your project is not aimed at you at all, thus reducing the potential for conflict because the third element is lacking.

Types of Conflicts

A distinction is generally made between task-related and people-related conflicts. The former involve disagreements over how to do a job (how to put the knives in the dishwasher, for example). Relational conflicts are about feelings of animosity or annoyance among people (for example, someone gets on your nerves because they talk too loudly on the phone). Contrary to popular belief, task-related conflicts can be just as harmful as relational conflicts. Although task-related conflicts can sometimes stimulate innovation or debate, they are also negatively related to employee job satisfaction and performance. Moreover, when we disagree on how to perform a task, we instinctively turn against our opponent. Task-related conflicts then quickly become people-related conflicts. Take the reactions of motorists involved in an accident. Insults are hurled, but no one analyses the situation to see who is really at fault in terms of traffic regulations. Specific aspects of relational conflicts (insults) thus appear on the fringes of a conflict purely related to the task (a driving error).

Temporal Dynamics of a Conflict

Conflicts are dynamic, meaning they evolve over time. At the outset, a conflict is *latent*. This is the case when all the contextual factors necessary for its emergence are present. A conflict reaches the stage of *perceived* when at least one person perceives that a potential conflict could emerge, and then *felt*, when at least one person experiences emotional states (anger, frustration, etc.) related to the conflict. However, it is only when at least one person expresses conflicting behavior (verbal or nonverbal aggression, sabotage, rumors, etc.) that the conflict becomes *manifest*.

As in the example of Alexander and Mia, it can be difficult for a leader to detect a conflict before it becomes manifest and truly expresses itself. Initially, it is a question of perception and feelings on the part of those involved. Then the conflict reaches a turning point. A vicious cycle develops, where each person takes the conflict one notch higher. Its intensity thus tends to increase exponentially, with the solutions diminishing inversely. Some researchers speak of "conflict escalation." This automatic negative spiral is characteristic of most conflict situations and begins with explicit disagreements leading to engaged discussions. Tensions then cause people to focus on aspects that divide, neglecting those that unite them. Opportunities for consensus disappear as both sides stick firmly to their views. If this polarization becomes more pronounced and entrenched, exchange will be seen as useless, and communication will be disrupted. The conflict worsens when it is fueled by explicit threats or direct attacks.

How to Deal with Conflict as a Leader?

For anyone in a leadership position, the goal is to act before the conflict gets out of control. Ideally, a leader should be able to spot the warning signs of an emerging conflict and prevent it from becoming manifest and escalating. These clues can be rumors, as in the example of Alexander and Mia, or unusual behavior (for example, two co-workers who no longer greet each other). Detecting a latent conflict is, of course, far from easy, and requires a great deal of sensitivity and interpretation. Listening skills (Chapter 5) and comprehension skills (Chapter 3) are essential for disarming the bomb before it explodes.

Failing that, action has to be taken once the conflict becomes manifest. As hostility can develop quickly, it is best to act at the first signs of explicit tension between collaborators. The leader's priority should be to re-establish contact and communication between staff members; a meeting to get things under control and try to find a solution is often a good way to do this. This meeting is typically carried out in three stages.

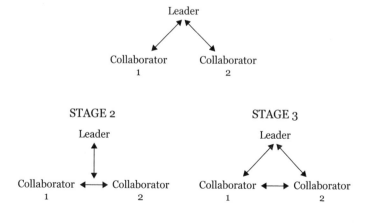

Stage 1

First of all, it is important to clarify the rules that need to be followed during the session. The most important rule is that the discussion must focus on behavior ("James insulted me") and not on the person ("James is incompetent"). This principle avoids personal attacks. Also, you must remind the collaborators not to interrupt each other so that they can hear each other's points of view.

The aim of this initial stage is to discuss "individually" with each employee in the presence of the other. This will allow them to express themselves freely and to discover how the other collaborator perceives the same situation. The aim of these initial exchanges is to identify the source of the conflict and the expectations of the parties regarding the resolution of the conflict. Here is an example of a session introduction based on Alexander and Mia's case:

> *You*: Good morning and thank you both for coming. I have asked you to this meeting in response to the rather heated exchange you've just had. First, I would like to understand what's going on so that we can work together to find a solution. To do that, I would like to start by hearing from you, one after the other. I don't want any personal scores to be settled. I would like you to focus on the behaviors that have upset you and that, in your opinion, have led to this conflict. Mia, can you start?

At this stage, it is important to use active listening techniques (Chapter 5) in order to best understand the views of the individual contributors. After listening to them, you will, with their help, prioritize the issues raised. The most important ones, that is, those that led directly to the conflict, should be addressed as a priority during the rest of the session.

Stage 2

The two employees will then be invited to talk between themselves and exchange their opinions. Here is how to introduce this second step:

> *You*: All right, thank you for sharing. So, if I understand correctly, the main problem is that you don't agree on how to manage the customer database. You, Mia, would like a weekly follow-up of the files, while you, Alexander, think that weekly is too often. Is that it?
>
> *Mia*: Yes, exactly...
>
> *Alexander*: Yes, that's right.
>
> *You*: OK, great. I would now like us to find solutions to the problem. What would you suggest?

The leader plays a facilitating role with the aim of encouraging the employees themselves to discuss and find solutions. The leader should continue to reformulate and clarify the collaborators' opinions in order to avoid potential misunderstandings or to get the dialogue back on track if they remain at loggerheads. It is important to maintain a solution-oriented mindset. In the event of a blocked exchange, communication can be resumed in the following way:

> *Mia*: Alexander, I can only repeat myself... We need to check the files more frequently! Once a week, minimum!
>
> *Alexander*: But are you aware of how much time that takes? To check files that most of the time don't even need to be changed? I am sorry, but we're already wasting too much time with those files; once a month is quite sufficient.
>
> *Mia*: Once a month? You've got to be joking...
>
> *(Long silence)*
>
> *You*: Listen, I realize that both of you are convinced you're right. But the purpose of this meeting is not to persuade the other that your point of view is the right one; the purpose is to find a solution that might work for both of you. You know, between once a week and once a month, there is a certain amount of leeway. Can we not find a compromise that would suit both of you?

During this stage, the leader will take note of the different ideas put forward and begin to think about solutions that might satisfy both sides.

Stage 3

Finally, the leader will conclude the discussion with a form of agreement between the employees. This will highlight what the solution can bring to each of them and will unite them rather than emphasize their different points of view. For example:

> *You*: Excellent. Do either of you want to add anything more? No? Thank you. From what I have gathered, the problem is not so much how often the files are being checked, but rather the way the checks are being done, right?
>
> *Alexander*: Yes, that's exactly it.
>
> *You*: Right, in that case, one suggestion could be to check over it together, so that any misunderstandings can be ruled out?
>
> *Mia*: Exactly.
>
> *You*: OK. So how would you proceed, concretely?

At such a meeting, the leader—and this is important—must remain neutral, not judge or take sides. This implies a mastery of both verbal and nonverbal behavior; even down to equally distributing your speaking time between the collaborators and making sure you look as much at one collaborator as at the other. Where each person is seated at the table is also important; the leader should position the employees face to face, in order to facilitate their exchanges, whereas the leader's position is at the side, at an equal distance from the stakeholders and without being more oriented toward one than the other.

As a final note, do not forget that if a conflict should get out of hand, it may become necessary to call on the services of experts in conflict resolution (professional mediators). It is part of a leader's responsibility to know when conflict management is beyond their own abilities.

10 How to Negotiate
An Interaction
with Four Principles

*As one of the sites of an American group special-
ized in the manufacture of construction machin-
ery is facing the loss of 733 jobs, five managers
of the company's Grenoble plant were taken hostage on Tuesday morning by employees on strike.*

This was a radio news broadcast describing the crisis situation at the Caterpillar plant in Grenoble on
March 31, 2009. This radical action was carried out by
plant workers after negotiations had failed. The objective of the hostage-taking? To resume negotiations with
management in order to increase severance payments
and reduce the number of layoffs from 733 to 450. This
example, as well as those of 3M and Sony a few weeks
earlier, shows that failed negotiations can have extreme
consequences.

Whether it is a matter of discussing with employees,
management, or third parties (suppliers, customers,
or competitors), leaders are constantly called upon to
negotiate. This also means that they are on the front-
line when a negotiation fails or ends in disagreement.

Knowing how to conduct a negotiation is therefore of paramount importance. When we talk about negotiation, we do not just mean that a person gets what they want, we mean achieving results that are fair and equitable for all parties at the table. It is not a question of altruism: the success of a negotiation has long-term effects. Reaching an agreement that harms one or more parties can open the door to possible retaliation, damage relations, or lead to conflict. The Treaty of Versailles, signed in June 1919, imposed unjust and excessively heavy sanctions on Germany and was one of the root causes of the Second World War.

Negotiation is a process of discussion between two or more parties with the aim of reaching an agreement. Your children haggle with you for the right to an hour of video games per day, your employees negotiate for a higher salary, and so on. Even though we are constantly exposed to situations of negotiation, it is still a difficult exercise that mixes cooperation and competition. All parties want to reach an agreement but have different interests. In this chapter, we will set out four basic principles for mastering the art of negotiation.

Transparency: Unfixing the Fixed Pie

The first difficulty in a negotiation process is that the majority of us tend to perceive the interests of the other party as diametrically opposed to our own. We therefore see negotiation as a "you win, I lose—you lose, I win" situation. This is called the fixed pie bias. We focus on one

particular aspect of the negotiation without consider-
ing other opportunities. Imagine for a moment that you
decide to buy a car. You have $30,000 but the model you
are interested in costs $35,000. If the seller only focuses
on the selling price, there is a good chance you won't
buy a car because he can't afford a $5,000 discount.
However, if he can understand that the color of the car
doesn't matter to you, he might be able to offer you the
canary yellow display model at a price that fits your budget—a model he has been trying to sell for months. You
don't care about the color and accept the offer.

The goal of any negotiation is therefore to cut the pie
into several pieces to satisfy everyone. Indeed, a negotiation does not simply consist of agreeing, for example, on
the price of a service. A negotiation often involves a range
of different elements to be negotiated. For an employment contract, we will not only talk about salary, but also
about potential bonuses, days off, or the possibility of tele-
working. The value of these elements can vary from one
person to another. For a young father, the possibility of
working from home one day a week may compensate for
a lower salary, but for a single person this may not be the
case. The leader's task is to identify and understand what
is important to the other person in order to prioritize and
evaluate the options before starting the negotiation.

This of course implies knowing the needs and expectations of the people you are dealing with. Several techniques are available, beginning, first of all, with active
listening. Listening attentively, asking questions, and
reformulating are essential for detecting the other

party's wishes as the negotiation progresses, because they sometimes reveal options that were not initially considered. Moreover, contrary to what people think, clearly communicating one's interests (the list of points to be negotiated and their priority) creates a climate of transparency that considerably optimizes the quality of an exchange and its chances of success. By explicitly expressing our motivations, the emergence of options is facilitated, as in the case of the price and color of the car. Be careful, however, not to confuse transparency of interests (that which is important to us) with transparency of room for negotiation (the minimum point beyond which you would no longer negotiate).

Reciprocity: Give to Receive

To illustrate the principle of reciprocity, imagine receiving an end-of-year greeting card from someone you don't know. Knowing that the sender's address is written on the card, what do you do? Do you ignore the card from this unknown sender or do you, in turn, wish this person happy holidays by sending them a card? If you are like 20 percent of the population, you will choose to send a card back. We have developed standards that govern part of our social behavior. For example, we teach our children to say "thank you" when they receive a gift. Reciprocity is based on a social norm of exchange in which we must give something equivalent in return for information, a service, or an object received, in order to level the playing field.

This principle of reciprocity explains why concessions are so important in negotiations. By agreeing to "give" something in return, you trigger a process of reciprocity: your counterpart is indebted to you and must compensate for this "debt" by making a concession. In a salary negotiation with an employee, you may agree to a lower employment rate or the possibility of training in exchange for a lower salary. So do not hesitate to make explicit concessions on aspects that you consider to be of minor importance in order to get the other party to in turn accept aspects that are perhaps more important to you.

Anchoring: Making the First Offer and Being Ambitious

In negotiations, a question often arises. Should I wait for the other party to make an offer before reacting, or is it better to reveal your cards first? Let's answer this question with the following example. You want to sell your house and, based on market prices, you hope to get $1,000,000. You're thinking of making a first offer of $1,100,000. However, in the negotiation process, if the buyer is the first to announce a price and offers $800,000, it becomes difficult for you to make a counter-offer close to your desired amount. This phenomenon is known as "anchor effect," where the first number proposed "attracts" all other offers like a magnet. This effect even strikes experts. In a study at the University of Arizona, for example, researchers asked real estate agents to estimate the value of a property objectively. All the agents obtained the same information and went to the property for an appraisal. However, half of the agents were advised of a higher listing price than the other half. The result? The agents themselves were influenced. The property, although identical for all agents, was valued at a higher price when the listing price was higher.

In order to use the anchor effect to your advantage, it is necessary to define three values before a negotiation starts: the optimal value (OV), indicating what you hope to achieve in the best case, the target value (TV), what you think you can actually achieve, and finally your BATNA—Best Alternative To a Negotiated Agreement—which can be understood as your "best alternative". The BATNA is the lower limit (if you are the seller) or the upper limit (if you are the buyer) beyond which you do not want to go. Setting a BATNA is essential for setting a limit to the negotiation, a threshold that will prevent you from accepting solutions that are too far from your target value. If we return to the previous example and the seller's point of view, the optimal value is \$1,000,000, the target value is \$975,000, and the BATNA is \$900,000. These three values are essential to help you define the first offer you are going to communicate which normally is higher than your optimal value, for example, \$1,100,000. The illustration below represents the three values for the buyer (TV1, OV1, BATNA1) and for the seller (TV2, OV2, BATNA2).

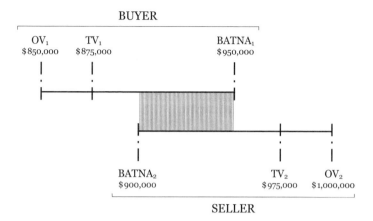

The objective of any negotiation is therefore to come as close as possible to your target value without exceeding the BATNA of the other party. Agreements are often located in the overlapping area of the two BATNAs (hatched in the illustration).

Liking: Similarity and Agreeableness

Have you ever noticed that if you get along well with another person, you tend to cross your arms at the same time, smile simultaneously, or sit in the chair in the same way? This imitation occurs when there is a link of sympathy. But is it possible to fake this connection? Can one appear more likeable in the eyes of the other person by knowingly imitating their behavior?

The answer is yes. As soon as you imitate the non-verbal behavior of your counterpart, they will tend to find you more likeable. As a negotiator, imitating the other person's nonverbal behavior is therefore an effective strategy. At least, this is what was highlighted in a study in which negotiators who mirrored their social interaction partners' mannerisms obtained better results.

It is important to note that in addition to appearing similar, it is necessary to appear pleasant in order to inspire liking. Continuing to smile during negotiations and not getting carried away by negative emotions (anger or frustration) are therefore key for keeping communication and cooperation going. Personal information can also be shared to create a good social relationship and maximize the chances of successful negotiation. In this regard, one study showed that participants were more likely to reach an agreement in an e-mail negotiation if the negotiation was based on a five-minute telephone discussion to get to know each other and if the negotiators saw a picture of the other party.

The table below summarizes the four strategies you can use, alone or in combination, to improve the chances of successful negotiation. These principles help not only to promote the emergence of an agreement but also to maintain a good relationship with your negotiating partners, which is essential when it comes to collaborators, for example.

Principles of negotiation	Negotiation strategy
Transparency	• Make a priority list of items to be negotiated • Share this list at the beginning of the negotiation process
Reciprocity	• Making concessions • Explicitly mention the concessions made
Anchoring	• Make the first offer • Be ambitious in your offer
Liking	• Mimicking the behavior of the other • Keep smiling and share information about yourself

11 Giving Constructive Feedback

Jacob is walking through the reception area of his retail agency when he notices that David, who is in charge of customer reception, is tapping away on his private mobile phone. A customer is patiently waiting for him to finish his message. Jacob thought he had made it clear that it is strictly forbidden to use private mobile phones in the presence of customers. His reaction is immediate. He approaches David furiously and yells at him, saying that his behavior is inacceptable and that the next time this happens, the HR department will be involved. Jennifer, who is taking care of another customer, hears everything. She discreetly watches the rest of the scene. David apologizes, stutters a few words of apology, and addresses the client with courtesy and no little embarrassment. That same evening at home, when Jacob recounts the story over dinner, the remarks of his wife and daughters make him realize that he may not have handled the incident in the best possible way. Was calling David to order in that way really the right thing to do? How would he have reacted if his immediate superior had given him such negative feedback in front of his colleagues and clients?

The purpose of this chapter is not to advise leaders to abandon negative remarks. On the contrary, it aims to give tips for how to successfully deliver negative feedback. As discussed in Chapter 6, feedback is one of the most effective ways for leaders to develop and motivate their employees.

Why Is Feedback So Important?

From the age of two, we are all "self-aware," meaning that we recognize ourselves as an individual distinct from our environment and the people surrounding us. The mirror test is a telling illustration of this phenomenon. Take a child, paint a red dot on the child's forehead (avoid permanent markers), and place the child in front of a mirror. Until the child becomes self-aware, they will see another child in front of them with a red mark on their forehead. However, as soon as the child is conscious of their own existence, they will understand who the reflection in the mirror is and will put their hand to their forehead to explore the strange red mark. This self-consciousness is not unique to the human species. Animals such as elephants, dolphins, and certain great apes also react to the mirror test. Why is self-awareness important? Because it gives rise to the very first feedback that we can receive: our own.

We can see ourselves as intelligent, funny, or extraverted, and we can be aware of some of our limitations when faced with certain tasks. When presenting in public, we may realize that we speak too softly or that we are not articulate enough. This observation is an initial feedback that can trigger efforts to improve. However, self-perception has its limits and does not necessarily correspond to how others perceive us. If we take the example of public speaking, you may think that you speak slowly, but actually your audience thinks that you speak too fast. In some cases, the differences between self-perception and perception-by-others are minimal, whereas in other cases, they can lead to major performance or comprehension problems.

When you want to develop your skills, the first step is to cross-examine your self-perception and the perceptions others have of you. Gaps will show underestimated strengths and ignored weaknesses.

It is the leader's responsibility to provide feedback to their subordinates in order for the latter to progress and develop. But how? Is it better to focus on the things that are going well and give positive feedback or to talk about what is problematic and give negative feedback? There is nothing obvious about this question. Too much positive feedback might lead to laziness and inertia, at least that is what many leaders fear. Too much criticism may discourage collaborators and reduce their willingness to improve. Science offers a nuanced answer: both forms of feedback can and should be used. The real challenge lies in the ability to communicate them appropriately.

How to Give Negative Feedback

Few people take pleasure in giving negative feedback. Leaders tend to avoid or distort criticism aimed at their collaborators. Similarly, few people enjoy receiving negative feedback. A completely unexpected reproach, pointing to a significant discrepancy between self-perception and perception-by-others, can lead to strong reactions such as anger or discouragement. Knowing when and how to give negative feedback is therefore necessary to avoid backlash. There are three rules for giving negative feedback that is effective in initiating behavior change in the co-worker while at the same time protecting their face.

1. *Control Your Emotions and Give Swift Feedback*

As in the example at the beginning of this chapter, we all tend to get angry at inappropriate behavior, especially when it is repeated. However, the first rule of negative feedback is to control your emotions! If you feel your neck tightening and your fists clenching, it's not the right time.

Wait for a moment, do some yoga, or just give yourself a few minutes until you calm down. When you've cooled down, it's time to address the incident, preferably in a private place away from prying eyes. But be careful not to wait too long. The closer the feedback is to the event, the more effective it will be. The problematic situation is still vivid in both your memory and that of the co-worker, which facilitates discussion and reduces the risk of misinterpretation. In Jacob's example, he should have talked to David in his office, quickly, but not on the spur of the moment.

2. Focus Feedback on Behavior

The second rule is to never criticize co-workers on a personal level. You need to focus on the behavior, the way a task has been performed. The aim is to point out the unacceptable behavior and why it is not tolerable, rather than to question the employee as a person. Statements such as "You are unprofessional!" or "Can't you do any better?" are ineffective and even counterproductive, as they are perceived as personal attacks. When self-esteem is affected, it cuts off any motivation to change, while at the same time damaging the quality of the relationship between the employee and the leader. The result is therefore opposite to what you wanted to achieve with the feedback.

3. Give Constructive Feedback

Although negative, criticism should always be constructive. To achieve this, here are three steps to follow. First, identify the problematic behavior explicitly and concretely. Second, explain the consequences of that behavior. Third, give the employee a chance to comment on their behavior. This sequence is essential to ensure that both the employee and the manager have all the information needed to establish that a problem exists and to discuss potential solutions. If Jacob had followed these steps, he would have learned that

David's wife was ill and that he was checking his messages because he was worried. Here's how Jacob might have talked to David:

"This morning, I saw that you responded to a text message on your phone in the presence of a client.

} 1) Description of the problematic behavior

You know that our clients deserve 100% of our attention if we want them to be satisfied.

} 2) Explanation of the consequences

Can you explain why you were on your phone instead of engaging with the customer?"

} 3) Opportunity to comment

Once the problematic behavior has been identified and both parties accept its problematic nature, it is time to consider solutions together. Jacob could, for example, have negotiated with David to only check his messages during the break, and that his wife could contact him directly on his business line in case of an emergency. Finally, negative feedback should always be accompanied by a final, positive comment in order to reaffirm the trust you have in your employee.

Communicating negative feedback in a constructive manner ensures that it is well received and that it will lead to performance improvements. It is important to note, however, that for a person who is totally immune to criticism, negative feedback will rarely lead to improvement, even if you master all the steps in the process.

Using the Annual Appraisal Interview to Develop and Motivate

Appraisal interviews are performance reviews in the form of periodic meetings (usually once a year). They are prepared in advance by the leader and provide an opportunity to review the events of the past period. The purpose of these interviews is to give feedback to employees. Usually, an appraisal interview is divided into two main phases: feedback on the employee's performance and setting future goals.

The first phase generally starts with the employee's own assessment of the period in question and their perspective on their performance. The leader's task in this phase is first and foremost to listen actively. It is also important to accept the nonlinear nature of the narrative, as the appraisal interview may concern more or less distant events that are sometimes difficult to place in a precise chronological order. You should therefore resist the temptation to interrupt the collaborator, even if you can see where they are going. The goal is to understand the perspective of the employee on their performance.

This step is crucial for both parties. On the one hand, the collaborator is given the opportunity to put into words how they perceive their work and their performance—in other words, to verbalize their self-perception. On the other hand, this narrative will allow the leader to complete their own picture of the employee with additional information and insights.

When the employee has finished detailing their personal assessment, it is the leader's turn to provide an assessment. This evaluation must be prepared in advance and can be supplemented by the information provided by the employee during the interview. This phase allows the employee to learn about the leader's point of view and to then cross-reference self-perception with perception-by-others. Don't hesitate to give a "sandwich" feedback, starting with the positive points, then gradually addressing the negative aspects, and concluding, once again, with some positive elements.

This exchange will serve as a basis for setting future objectives, particularly in terms of personal development. The differences between the employee's self-perception and the leader's perception are, by nature, good points for development. When it comes to objectives, it is essential not to lose sight of the motivational aspect and the SMART dimension of the agreed-upon goal for the future.

12 Your Leaderspritz

Anthony didn't see the day go by. The communication and leadership training offered by his company has already come to an end. As of tomorrow, he will be back in his department and back to his daily obligations—as well as his problems. This return to reality may quickly make or break the concepts and tools discovered in training. If we compare learning leadership skills to an iceberg, a course or reading a book is only the tip of the iceberg. The submerged part? The implementation of these recommendations in daily life. This final chapter will provide advice on how to continue developing your interpersonal leadership skills once you close this book.

Starting Point

When developing leadership skills, the first step is to establish the status quo, requiring you to identify personal strengths and weaknesses. There are several methods to assess your skills, but a checklist will instantly highlight how you perceive your skills. The checklist below will allow you to make this diagnosis in relation to the aspects discussed in the previous chapters. (Needless to say, its utility will depend entirely on your honesty when answering.)

Public presentations Importance: 1 2 3 4 5	Novice	Medium	Expert
I prepare my presentations around one or a few clearly identifiable key messages.			
I tend to occupy the space when I speak in public.			
I often use stories and metaphors in my presentations.			
I don't have a monotonous voice when I speak in public.			
I adapt my language (acronyms, vocabulary) according to the audience I am addressing.			
Managing meetings Importance: 1 2 3 4 5	Novice	Medium	Expert
I set specific goals for each meeting I organize.			
I make sure that everyone at the meeting is there for a reason.			
I pay particular attention to the quality of the physical environment (light, temperature, etc.) in the rooms in which I hold meetings.			
During a meeting, I try to allocate adequate speaking time to all those present.			
When I organize a meeting, I plan its duration in advance.			
Conflict management Importance: 1 2 3 4 5	Novice	Medium	Expert
I generally pay attention to signs of possible conflict between my collaborators (e.g., rumors).			
When I witness tension between certain collaborators, I react as quickly as possible to avoid the emergence of a greater conflict.			
During a conflict, I summon the collaborators involved to help them find a solution.			
I make sure not to judge my collaborators and to be as neutral as possible when I manage a conflict.			
If a conflict is beyond my control, I call upon an expert in conflict resolution, if necessary, from outside the company.			

Negotiation skills Importance: 1 2 3 4 5	Novice	Medium	Expert
I know my limits at the beginning of every negotiation.			
When I negotiate, I don't hesitate to make concessions on aspects that are not important to me.			
I tend to always make the first offer when I start a negotiation.			
When I negotiate, I remain pleasant in all circumstances.			
When I negotiate, I pay attention to the nonverbal behavior of the other party so that I can imitate it.			
Providing feedback Importance: 1 2 3 4 5	Novice	Medium	Expert
When I see an employee make a mistake, I summon them as soon as possible to talk to them about it.			
When I have to criticize one of my employees, I make sure to keep my emotions under control.			
When I give feedback to my collaborators, I focus on the behaviors that are problematic rather than on their personality.			
I always give my employees the opportunity to express themselves after giving them negative feedback.			
When I give negative feedback to my employees, I always end with a positive aspect.			

Defining the status quo offers several advantages. First, it allows you to establish a list of priorities and to focus your attention (and therefore your time) on the competencies you deem most important to develop. Second, it allows you to measure the success of your efforts based on a before/after comparison. Third, it provides an incentive to set realistic goals and, in some cases, to come up with ideas for improvement.

Prioritize

Once your self-diagnosis is complete, it is essential to rank the skills to be developed in order of importance. This step is critical in defining where to focus your energy. If you are in a leadership position, your professional responsibilities will occupy the majority of your agenda. Add to this a private life with its share of obligations, and the time available for self-development slips away very quickly. You need to spend these precious moments working on the skills that are critical to your success as a leader. We invite you to note how important each of the five aspects mentioned in the checklist above is for your daily activities as a leader, ranking them from 1 (major importance) to 5 (minor importance).

Plan

Once completed, the above checklist provides two pieces of information: a self-diagnosis of skills and their ranking in order of importance. These two pieces of information are essential to determine the next steps in your personal development. A common mistake is to start with the skills you consider yourself a novice in. This strategy is only effective if that skill is relevant to you. In some cases, it is better to try to become an "expert" in a skill that is essential to your job than to try to stop being "novice" in a skill that is ultimately of little importance to your daily activities.

Knowing this, it is now time to plan your personal development by choosing the skills to work on (the "what"), the goals to achieve, and the strategies to achieve them (the "how"). This planning will allow you to draw up a roadmap of your development project and maximize the chances of achieving your objectives.

There are a few tips for establishing an effective development plan. First, avoid working on all skills at the same time (practicing public speaking and learning how to give feedback, for example, could be more than enough to get you started). In some cases, a single skill will suffice. The next step is to set yourself SMART goals. It is particularly important that they are measurable and time-based to assess the success or failure of your work. If you are looking to improve your public speaking skills, you may, for example, set yourself the goal of giving three presentations during the upcoming year to gradually increase your presentation skills. You can also ask for feedback from the audience on your performance to quantify your progress. Finally, the third step is to choose strategies to achieve your objectives. They must be concrete and take into account both financial and organizational constraints. You could, for example, opt for a voice acting or public speaking course (provided it fits into your company's training budget) or invest two hours per week in the month preceding a speech to prepare it at all levels (structural, verbal, and nonverbal). Online courses are also an interesting option, since they offer good value for money.

The various elements of this planning (skills to be improved, objectives, strategies, and resources needed) must then be carried forward into a personal development plan. You can immediately start this reflection by means of the plan below (the first part, "Competence No. 1," will give an example).

Competence no. 1: Public speaking	
Objective: Prepare my end-of-year speech.	**Planned for:** In 6 months
Strategy no. 1: Sign up for a public speaking training course.	**Resources necessary:** Budget for training course.
Strategy no. 2: Practice regularly 5 weeks prior to the event.	**Resources necessary:** Put aside one hour per week to practice.

Competence no. 2:	
Objective:	**Planned for:**
Strategy no. 1:	**Resources necessary:**
Strategy no. 2:	**Resources necessary:**

Reality Check

Once the learning goals and strategies have been clearly established, the feasibility of your plan should be assessed. One of the most common mistakes when writing a personal development plan is to overestimate one's capacities (temporal, financial, and motivational) and to underestimate the constraints imposed by the environment. Anthony might want to practice public speaking for one hour a day, but he underestimates the time he spends with his children and wife when he gets home. Never forget that it is better to set smaller goals for which you are sure you have the resources, rather than setting unattainable goals that will only have one consequence—demotivate you. The reality check therefore entails comparing the resources needed to achieve the goal you have set for yourself with the constraints imposed by your environment.

Involve the People Around You

As we have seen in this book, being a leader is first and foremost about managing people, and therefore acquiring interpersonal skills. There is, therefore, a high probability that the goals and strategies set will involve those around you, whether professional or private. Of course, you can resort to a few tricks such as talking to a mirror or filming yourself, but you risk quickly becoming bored and your progress stagnating. Involving those around you is an important step in a personal development plan. It is essential that you know how to motivate those who will have to listen to you again and again—and who will also be the ones giving you feedback on how you communicate.

Practice

Armed with a personal development plan, as well as the concepts and tools discussed in this book, you are like a bartender faced with an empty glass and a multitude of ingredients. It's time for you to mix all these ingredients and become the leader you want to be. It's time for you to close this book and experiment with your new interpersonal skills. It's time for you to create your own cocktail! So, go ahead... it's up to you to shake it and find the best mix: yours!

References

1 Why Are Leaders Important?

Scientific papers

Darioly, A., & Schmid Mast, M. (2011). Facing an incompetent leader: The effects of a nonexpert leader on subordinates' perception and behaviour. *European Journal of Work and Organizational Psychology, 20*(2), 239–265.

Darley, J. M., & Latane, B. (1968). Bystander intervention in emergencies: Diffusion of responsibility. *Journal of Personality and Social Psychology, 8*(4), 377–383.

Kalma, A. (1991). Hierarchisation and dominance assessment at first glance. *European Journal of Social Psychology, 21*(2), 165–181.

2 The Fourteen-Billion-Dollar Question

Scientific papers

Antonakis, J., Fenley, M., & Liechti, S. (2011). Can charisma be taught? Tests of two interventions. *The Academy of Management Learning and Education, 10*(3), 374–396.

Judge, T. A., Bono, J. E., Ilies, R., & Gerhardt, M. W. (2002). Personality and leadership: A qualitative and quantitative review. *Journal of Applied Psychology, 87*(4), 765–780.

Judge, T. A., Colbert, A. E., & Ilies, R. (2004). A meta-analysis of the relationship between intelligence and leadership. *Journal of Applied Psychology, 89*(3), 542–552.

Kotter, J. P. (1999). *John P. Kotter on What Leaders Really Do.* Boston, MA: Harvard Business Review Book.

Luthans, F., Rosenkrantz, S. A., & Hennessey, H. W. (1985). What do successful managers really do? An observation study of managerial activities. *The Journal of Applied Behavioral Science, 21*(3), 255–270.

Mintzberg, H. (1973). *The Nature of Managerial Work.* New York: Harper & Row.

Other sources

Numbers regarding spending on training: O'Leonard, K. (2014). *The Corporate Learning Factbook 2014: Benchmarks, Trends, and Analysis of the U.S. Training Market.* Retrieved from: http://www.cedmaeurope.org/newsletter%20articles/ Brandon%20Hall/The%20Corporate%20Learning%20 Factbook%202014%20(Jan%2014).pdf

3 The Science of Communication

Scientific papers

Blanch-Hartigan, D., Andrzejewski, S. A., & Hill, K. M. (2012). The effectiveness of training to improve person perception accuracy: A meta-analysis. *Basic and Applied Social Psychology, 34*(6), 483–498.

Brunswik, E. (1956). *Perception and the Representative Design of Psychological Experiments.* Berkeley, CA: University of California Press.

Dovidio, J. F., & Ellyson, S. L. (1985). Patterns of visual dominance behavior in humans. In S. L. Ellyson & J. F. Dovidio (Eds.), *Power, Dominance, and Nonverbal Behavior,* 129–149. New York: Springer-Verlag.

Ekman, P., & O'Sullivan, M. (1991). Who can catch a liar? *American Psychologist, 46*(9), 913–920.

Hall, J. A., Andrzejewski, S. A., & Yopchick, J. E. (2009). Psychosocial correlates of interpersonal sensitivity: A meta-analysis. *Journal of Nonverbal Behavior, 33*(3), 149–180.

Hall, J. A., Coats, E. J., & LeBeau, L. S. (2005). Nonverbal behavior and the vertical dimension of social relations: A meta-analysis. *Psychological Bulletin, 131*(6), 898–924.

Hall, J. A., Schmid Mast, M., & West, T. V. (Eds.). (2016). *The Social Psychology of Perceiving Others Accurately.* Cambridge: Cambridge University Press.

Schmid Mast, M., & Hall, J. A. (2018). The impact of interpersonal accuracy for behavioral outcomes. *Current Directions in Psychological Science, 27*(5), 309–314.

Other sources

John Yarbrough's story: Gladwell, M. (2002, August 2). The naked face. *The New Yorker.* Retrieved from: https://www.newyorker.com

4 Can We Trust Our Brains?
Heuristics and Stereotypes

Scientific papers

Bell, S. T., Villado, A. J., Lukasik, M. A., Belau, L., & Briggs, A. L. (2011). Getting specific about demographic diversity variable and team performance relationships: A meta-analysis. *Journal of Management, 37*(3), 709–743.

Correll, J., Park, B., Judd, C. M., & Wittenbrink, B. (2002). The police officer's dilemma: Using ethnicity to disambiguate potentially threatening individuals. *Journal of Personality and Social Psychology, 83*(6), 1314–1329.

Devine, P. G. (1989). Stereotypes and prejudice: Their automatic and controlled components. *Journal of Personality and Social Psychology, 56*(1), 5–18.

Goldin, C., & Rouse, C. (2000). Orchestrating impartiality: The impact of "blind" auditions on female musicians. *American Economic Review, 90*(4), 715–741.

Rosenthal, R., & Jacobson, L. (1968). Pygmalion in the classroom. *The Urban Review, 3*(1), 16–20.

Schein, V. E., Mueller, R., Lituchy, T., & Liu, J. (1996). Think manager—think male: A global phenomenon? *Journal of Organizational Behavior, 17*(1), 33–41.

Schmid Mast, M. (2002). Dominance as expressed and inferred through speaking time: A meta-analysis. *Human Communication Research, 28*(3), 420–450.

Other sources

Riddle of the surgeon: Barlow, K. (2014, January 16). BU research: A riddle reveals depth of gender bias. *BU Today*. Retrieved from: https://www.bu.edu/today/2014/bu-research-riddle-reveals-the-depth-of-gender-bias/

5 Listening Skills

Scientific papers

Bodie, G. D. (2012). Listening as positive communication. In T. Socha & M. Pitts (Eds.), *The Positive Side of Interpersonal Communication*, 109–125. New York: Peter Lang.

Daimler, M. (2016). Listening is an overlooked leadership tool. *Harvard Business Review*. Retrieved from: https://hbr.org/2016/05/listening-is-an-overlooked-leadership-tool

Mayfield, J., & Mayfield, M. (2002). Leader communication strategies critical paths to improving employee commitment. *American Business Review, 20*(2), 89–94.

Minozzi W., C. G. (2015). Social influence in the House of representatives, 1801–1861. Paper presented at the Congress &

History Conference Vanderbilt University. Retrieved from: https://www.vanderbilt.edu/csdi/events/congress-history-conference-2015.php

Ng, T. W., & Feldman, D. C. (2012). Employee voice behavior: A meta-analytic test of the conservation of resources framework. *Journal of Organizational Behavior, 33*(2), 216–234.

O'Connor, P., Campbell, J., Newon, J., Melton, J., Salas, E., & Wilson, K. A. (2008). Crew resource management training effectiveness: A meta-analysis and some critical needs. *The International Journal of Aviation Psychology, 18*(4), 353–368.

Risser, D. T., Rice, M. M., Salisbury, M. L., Simon, R., Jay, G. D., & Berns, S. D. (1999). The potential for improved teamwork to reduce medical errors in the emergency department. *Annals of Emergency Medicine, 34*(3), 373–383.

Tost, L. P., Gino, F., & Larrick, R. P. (2012). Power, competitiveness, and advice taking: Why the powerful don't listen. *Organizational Behavior and Human Decision Processes, 117*(1), 53–65.

Other sources

Tenerife Crash. Retrieved from: https://www.youtube.com/watch?v=36XzwJqo_tg

Bhopal Disaster. Retrieved from: https://en.wikipedia.org/wiki/Bhopal_disaster

Greenville Accident: National Transportation Safety Board. *Marine Accident Brief.* Retrieved from: https://www.ntsb.gov/investigations/AccidentReports/Reports/MAB0501.pdf

6 Being a Good Leader

Scientific papers

Bass, B. M., Avolio, B. J., & Atwater, L. (1996). The transformational and transactional leadership of men and women. *Applied Psychology, 45*(1), 5–34.

Judge, T. A., & Piccolo, R. F. (2004). Transformational and transactional leadership: A meta-analytic test of their relative validity. *Journal of Applied Psychology, 89*(5), 755–768.

Locke, E. A. (1968). Toward a theory of task motivation and incentives. *Organizational Behavior and Human Performance, 3*(2), 157–189.

Palese, T., & Schmid Mast, M. (2018). Leadership flexibility: A double edged sword for leaders. Working paper.

Robbins, S. P., & Judge, T. A. (2011). *Organizational Behavior*. Upper Saddle River, NJ: Pearson.

Other sources

Concerning Ernest Shackleton: Sir Ernest Shackleton. Retrieved from: http://www.ernestshackleton.net/#about

https://en.wikipedia.org/wiki/Ernest_Shackleton

7 How to Give a Killer Presentation

Scientific papers

Antonakis, J., Fenley, M., & Liechti, S. (2011). Can charisma be taught? Tests of two interventions. *The Academy of Management Learning and Education, 10*(3), 374–396.

Gilovich, T., Savitsky, K., & Medvec, V. H. (1998). The illusion of transparency: Biased assessments of others' ability to read one's emotional states. *Journal of Personality and Social Psychology, 75*(2), 332–346.

Naftulin, D. H., Ware, J. E., & Donnelly, F. A. (1973). The Doctor Fox lecture: A paradigm of educational seduction. *Journal of Medical Education, 48*(7), 630–635.

Schmid, P. C., & Schmid Mast, M. (2013). Power increases performance in a social evaluation situation as a result of decreased stress responses. *European Journal of Social Psychology, 43*(3), 201–211.

Other sources

Structuring a speech: Morgan, N. (2001, February 2). *5 Quick Ways to Structure a Speech.* Retrieved from: https://www.publicwords.com/2011/02/02/5-quick-ways-to-structure-a-speech/

8 How to Organize an Effective Meeting

Scientific papers

Ariely, D., Kamenica, E., & Prelec, D. (2008). Man's search for meaning: The case of Legos. *Journal of Economic Behavior & Organization, 67*(3-4), 671–677.

Baron, R. A. (1972). Aggression as a function of ambient temperature and prior anger arousal. *Journal of Personality and Social Psychology, 21*(2), 183–189.

Cohen, M. A., Rogelberg, S. G., Allen, J. A., & Luong, A. (2011). Meeting design characteristics and attendee perceptions of staff/team meeting quality. *Group Dynamics: Theory, Research, and Practice, 15*(1), 90–104.

Luong, A., & Rogelberg, S. G. (2005). Meetings and more meetings: The relationship between meeting load and the daily well-being of employees. *Group Dynamics: Theory, Research, and Practice, 9*(1), 58–67.

Mosvick, R. K., & Nelson, R. B. (1987). *We've Got to Start Meeting Like This! A Guide to Successful Business Meeting Management.* Glenview, IL: Scott, Foresman and Co.

Van Vree, W. (1999). *Meetings, Manners, and Civilization: The Development of Modern Meeting Behaviour.* London: Leicester University Press.

Other sources

Statistics on meetings in the US: Verizon. *A Study of Trends, Costs, and Attitudes Toward Business Travel and Teleconferencing, and Their Impact on Productivity.* Retrieved from: https://emeetings.verizonbusiness.com/global/en/meetingsinamerica/uswhitepaper.php

9 How to Manage Conflicts: A Lesson in Diplomacy

Scientific papers

De Dreu, C. K., & Weingart, L. R. (2003). Task versus relationship conflict, team performance, and team member satisfaction: A meta-analysis. *Journal of Applied Psychology, 88*(4), 741–749.

Jehn, K. A. (1995). A multimethod examination of the benefits and detriments of intragroup conflict. *Administrative Science Quarterly, 40*(2), 256–282.

Pondy, L. R. (1967). Organizational conflict: Concepts and models. *Administrative Science Quarterly, 12*(2), 296–320.

Rubin, J. Z., Pruitt, D. G., & Kim, S. H. (1994). *Social Conflict: Escalation, Stalemate, and Settlement.* New York: McGraw-Hill Book Company.

Thomas, K. W. (1992). Conflict and negotiation processes in organizations. In M. D. Dunnette & L. M. Hough (Eds.),

Handbook of Industrial and Organizational Psychology, 651–701. Palo Alto, CA: Consulting Psychologists Press.

Tschan, F., Messerli, L., Kings, F., & Amaretti, M. (2006). Prevalence of emotions experienced in everyday interactions. Paper presented at the Proceedings of the first Annual Report, NCCR Affective Sciences.

10 How to Negotiate: An Interaction with Four Principles

Scientific papers

Barry, B., Lewicki, R. J., & Saunders, D. M. (2011). *Essentials of negotiation*. New York: McGraw-Hill Higher Education.

De Dreu, C. K., Koole, S. L., & Steinel, W. (2000). Unfixing the fixed pie: A motivated information-processing approach to integrative negotiation. *Journal of Personality and Social Psychology, 79*(6), 975–987.

Galinsky, A. D., & Mussweiler, T. (2001). First offers as anchors: The role of perspective-taking and negotiator focus. *Journal of Personality and Social Psychology, 81*(4), 657–669.

Gouldner, A. W. (1960). The norm of reciprocity: A preliminary statement. *American Sociological Review, 25*(2), 161–178.

Kunz, P. R., & Woolcott, M. (1976). Season's greetings: From my status to yours. *Social Science Research, 5*(3), 269–278.

Maddux, W. W., Mullen, E., & Galinsky, A. D. (2008). Chameleons bake bigger pies and take bigger pieces: Strategic behavioral mimicry facilitates negotiation outcomes. *Journal of Experimental Social Psychology, 44*(2), 461–468.

Mehu, M., Grammer, K., & Dunbar, R. I. (2007). Smiles when sharing. *Evolution and Human Behavior, 28*(6), 415–422.

Morris, M., Nadler, J., Kurtzberg, T., & Thompson, L. (2002). Schmooze or lose: Social friction and lubrication in e-mail negotiations. *Group Dynamics: Theory, Research, and Practice, 6*(1), 89–100.

Northcraft, G. B., & Neale, M. A. (1987). Experts, amateurs, and real estate: An anchoring-and-adjustment perspective on property pricing decisions. *Organizational Behavior and Human Decision Processes, 39*(1), 84–97.

Rackham, N., & Carlisle, J. (1978). The effective negotiator— Part I: The behaviour of successful negotiators. *Journal of European Industrial Training, 2*(6), 6–11.

Thompson, L., & Hastie, R. (1990). Social perception in negotiation. *Organizational Behavior and Human Decision Processes, 47*(1), 98–123.

Other sources

Caterpillar strike: Europe 1 (2009, 18 mars). Grenoble: 4 leaders held hostage. *Le Journal du dimanche*. Retrieved from: https://www.lejdd.fr/Societe/Grenoble-4-dirigeants-sequestres-75195-3075500

11 Giving Constructive Criticism

Scientific papers

Amsterdam, B. (1972). Mirror self-image reactions before age two. *Developmental Psychobiology, 5*(4), 297–305.

Benedict, M. E., & Levine, E. L. (1988). Delay and distortion: Tacit influences on performance appraisal effectiveness. *Journal of Applied Psychology, 73*(3), 507–514.

Kluger, A. N., & DeNisi, A. (1996). The effects of feedback interventions on performance: A historical review, a meta-analysis, and a preliminary feedback intervention theory. *Psychological Bulletin, 119*(2), 254–284.

Brett, J. F., & Atwater, L. E. (2001). 360° feedback: Accuracy, reactions, and perceptions of usefulness. *Journal of Applied Psychology, 86*(5), 930–942.

Steelman, L. A., & Rutkowski, K. A. (2004). Moderators of employee reactions to negative feedback. *Journal of Managerial Psychology, 19*(1), 6–18.

The Authors

Marianne Schmid Mast is full professor of organizational behavior at the Faculty of Economics and Business (HEC) at the University of Lausanne. After obtaining her doctorate in Psychology from the University of Zurich, she continued her research at Northeastern University in Boston (USA). She was then assistant professor in social psychology at the University of Fribourg and then full professor at the Institute for Work and Organizational Psychology at the University of Neuchâtel. Her research focuses on the ways in which individuals interact within hierarchies, perceive and communicate (verbally and nonverbally), how first impressions affect interpersonal interactions and evaluations, and how individuals form correct first impressions of others. She is the author of more than 100 scientific publications and is currently an associate editor for the *Journal of Nonverbal Behavior*. She also serves on the editorial board of the journal *Leadership Quarterly*. She is a former member of the board of the Swiss National Science Foundation and was president of the Swiss Psychological Society. She is a Fellow of the Society for Social and Personality Psychology (SPSP) and a Fellow Division 8 of the American Psychological Association (APA), in honor of her extraordinary, distinctive, and ongoing contributions to social and personality psychology. In 2018 and in 2019, she was named one of the 50 most influential living psychologists in the world (thebestschools.org).

Tristan Palese holds a doctorate in management from the Faculty of Economics and Business (HEC) at the University of Lausanne. His research focuses mainly on the importance of social skills for managers. He holds a bachelor's degree in psychology from the University of Geneva and a master's degree in work and organizational psychology from the University of Neuchâtel. His professional career has led him to present his research at international conferences of experts and to participate in various training courses related to management. Passionate about teaching, he is particularly interested in disseminating knowledge from the world of research in order to make it accessible to as many people as possible. Today, he works in a public hospital as a training officer and teaches courses at university level.

Benjamin Tur holds a doctorate in management from the Faculty of Economics and Business (HEC) at the University of Lausanne. His research focuses on leadership, charisma, and their effects on individuals. In particular, his work deals with the types of verbal and nonverbal behaviors that are perceived as charismatic. He teaches charisma for managers and in a digital course available on the website www.leaderspritz.com. In addition to his work on leadership, Benjamin Tur has a strong experience in finance. He has worked in mergers and acquisitions, in financial advisory for a large private bank, and is currently managing a wealth management firm.